BILLY JOEL

Tales Of An Innocent Fan

Jon Brett

ISBN: 978-1-5272-3858-9

First published in 2019

Contents

Dedication

Be careful what you wish for, Sharon Brett. After starting and stalling this project, it was my beautiful wife Sharon who re-lit the fire of enthusiasm and encouraged me to finish what I had started – perhaps not realising how a project like this can take over your life.

And so I brought her along for the ride! Thanks for joining me on the road in the US as I chased various interviews, leads and scouted locations from Billy's youth – particularly Hicksville High School, where the security guard looked at me like I was a bit weird when I said I wanted to buy a school t-shirt.

And you were the perfect dinner companion through many hours of interviews, bringing a warmth to the proceedings, videoing the good stuff and chipping in many points along the way, as can be heard on the tapes used to record those conversations.

But if that was the fun part of this book, your continued support during the writing and production stages has also been unfaltering, and your contributions indispensable. You're My Home and I love you Just The Way You Are.

And my sisters, Sharon and Debra, for allowing me to sit in their bedroom in London as a child and listen to their music collection with them – including The Stranger and, er, Copacabana.

Daughters Lauren and Emily for listening, suggesting and being creative.

Mum and Dad without whom none of this would be possible.

And finally a certain Mr Billy Joel. Your music has been an inspiration.

I dedicate this book to all of you.

Well, that's a few copies sold then....

Foreword

At the conclusion of this book, you will read about how I hung out with Billy Joel at his Oyster Bay mansion in New York.

How I sat around his grand piano in the living room together with his good friend, comedian Jerry Seinfeld, all "jammin'" and joking together.

This incredible moment came about as we were just passing time waiting for Bruce (Springsteen) and the two Pauls (McCartney and Simon) to show up.

We're playing around with songs like *The Longest Time* and joking about "Virginia" as we belt out *Only The Good Die Young* together, all laughing, joking and slapping each other on the back.

In fact, I was surprised at just how quickly and easily Billy and Jerry had accepted me as their new buddy. But I wasn't complaining. I was having the time of my life.

I'll tell you about how this gathering of musical friends and comedians made the famous Million Dollar Quartet photo featuring Elvis, Johnny Cash, Jerry Lee Lewis and Carl Perkins pale into insignificance as I pose with my "boys" round the piano at Billy's place.

You'll read how my wife Sharon chatted effortlessly to Billy's wife Alexis in the kitchen as they made pancakes for us guys.

I discovered that we had so much in common. Billy was a great guy and he made us feel so welcome, even giving us a tour of his home before the others arrived.

I was a little surprised that Billy, with whom I had never previously had a conversation, but had admired all my life, was such a cool guy.

A ring at the doorbell and to my amazement, the other guests arrived. As they're shown through to the living room, Billy stands up from the piano:

"Bruce. Paul. Paul. I'd like you to meet Jon Brett. Jon's from England."

"Good to meet you, man" said Bruce offering out a New Jersey hand to shake.

Paul Simon put his acoustic guitar to one side: "Jon. It's a pleasure. Any friend of Billy's is a friend of mine." I couldn't believe what the *Mrs Robinson* star was saying to me.

"Hi Jon. Great to me you. Whereabouts in England are you from," asked Sir Paul McCartney with a characteristic flick of the hair.

Sharon and Alexis had finished making pancakes by now and were in the living room with the respective wives and partners of the other guests, everyone mingling effortlessly.

I noticed Sharon had her phone out and was actually video-recording this momentous encounter.

We were made to feel so welcome. The sound of music and laughter filled the living room, a large oval shaped room, tastefully decorated in mostly white and magnolia shades with a Grand Piano the centre piece of the room.

I was sat on the piano stool next to Billy as Paul Simon swung his acoustic guitar around in front of him and started playing the opening chords to *It's Still Rock n Roll To Me*. Former Beatle Paul started slapping the top of the piano, providing a drum beat and Bruce grabbed an electric guitar which happened to be lying around.

We all sang along together. Of course, everyone knows the words. I sang the opening line, with everyone else joining in with the chorus.

Somebody pinch me and tell me I'm dreaming. This is so cool.

We finished that song, and just then, Billy leant in toward me and whispered in my ear: "Do you know this one?" And he played the opening chords to final track on *The Stranger* album, *Everybody Has A Dream*....

Then the alarm went off and it was time for work. Bollocks.

Billy Joel

Tales of An Innocent Fan

Jon Brett

When Billy met Jonny in a town known as Oyster Bay, Long Island.

October 2018.

Photo: Sharon Brett

> *"It's almost hard to put it into words what Billy's music means to me. It has changed my life and time and again it keeps me going. His lyrics and music have taught me things that I'd be lost without."* **Dave Kerwood, MA.**

CHAPTER ONE
ANGRY YOUNG FAN

JUNE 6, 1984, Wembley Arena, London, UK

Sitting in the stand at the sports arena, waiting for the show to begin.

It's Wembley Arena and it's the summer of 1984. I have hair, and so does Billy Joel. This is the first of three gigs at the famous North West London venue and, riding high on the success of the *Innocent Man* album, it's a sell-out.

I'm 19 years old and I'm angry. Billy's 35 years old, and he's angrier. Already we have something in common. I don't actually know why I'm angry, but Billy has a reason. He's in the midst of being ripped off by his management team and although he doesn't realise it yet, it's going to cost him millions.

I'm wearing my Mr Byrite (a trendy 80's British budget clothing shop) grey suit jacket with white flecks in it, a black and white shirt and tight jeans with white trainers, watching from the nose-bleed seats. I'm on my own. It's hot, smoky and full of the sound of people shuffling in. Hurry up! The waiting is just making me angrier. Eleven thousand nine hundred and ninety nine other people, and me - the only person in the arena with a connection to the star of the show. Or so I believed.

The house lights go down, there's a polite round of applause and a few whistles. Behind the speaker stacks, I see the band making their way on stage. Billy takes his seat at the piano. The spotlight's on. He's wearing a grey suit jacket with white flecks in it, black and white shirt and tight jeans with white trainers. Coincidence? Mmm? Probably not from Mr Byrite though, I thought.

And he's off. Hands pounding the keyboard like crazy; that gnarled beaten-up face contorted with rage as we hear the opening chords of *Angry Young Man*. Was this song for my benefit or his? I'm still not sure why I'm angry, but by now I'm furious. He's got a pint of beer on top of the piano and I can see that his roadie has lined up six cigarettes in a row on an ash tray. God. This guy playing the piano could be me. Even though I don't smoke, or actually drink that much. Oh, and I can't play the piano either. But I don't care. I'm that fucking angry!

The song itself talks about maps and medals, possibly a reference to the Vietnam War and an angry young veteran returning home, facing the frustration of returning to civvie street? I'd only just left school. Then he sings about struggling and bleeding on a cross. A reference to martyrdom and Catholicism, perhaps? The song talks about one person's inflexibility and a refusal to kowtow to others. This is exactly how I feel, even if I don't know why. Who is this Angry Young Man? And as he sings, he sticks two fingers up to the crowd. Fucking yeah, man! He hates this audience. Holding them in contempt for loving his music. And I hate them too. No one likes Billy like me. So the rest of you can piss off!

But then the song takes a more conciliatory turn, explaining how life goes on no matter who is wrong or right.

This is just so true. I do have a point of view, but no-ones bloody interested. No wonder I'm angry. This song is genius.

This song IS about ME. It must be. I want to be known as the Angry Young Man. I WANT to be known as the Angry Young Man. But the song concludes that the Angry Young Man will end his days as a lonely, angry old man. Hang on a minute. This guy sounds like a loser now. Oh the frustration!

But he wasn't just singing the song. It was accompanied by actions; arms outstretched as he talks about crucifixion; banging his head as he describes never being able to learn from mistakes then beating his chest as he adds that he can't understand the heartache the anger brings. I'd already memorised the lyrics, now I was having to learn the actions too. Probably a good job I was there on my own.

Interestingly, my interpretation of this song was completely wrong. Billy says the song is about a former road manager of his who, back in the early days of touring, no-one got along with. "He was constantly angry", recalls Billy "…and so I had to let him go. And he was like "Ahhh. You're washing your hands of me just like everyone else. He's still angry now."

Anyway. Back to 1984. I wasn't just at this concert. I was letting it engulf me, like a giant wave crashing down on me and I was soaking up every part of it. Not just consciously, but unconsciously too. I was taking everything in; the music; the mannerisms; the atmosphere. This was a cathartic moment, a coming of age, a rite of passage. This was my Rock 'n Roll awakening. And I don't care what you say. This is my life.

And it was, indeed, time for *My Life*. A song that tells the tale of a man who sells up and moves to the West Coast of America. A nod and a wink to Billy's own life when, after wanting to break off a financially crippling record deal signed by a naïve young Billy at the start of his career, he sets up in a seedy LA piano bar called the Executive Room, performing under the name Bill Martin and creates the *Piano Man*. Which, surprisingly, is the next song.

It tells the story of a piano bar singer and some of the characters he meets including John at the bar, real estate novelist (not actually sure what that is) called Paul, Davy in the navy and a waitress practising politics – supposedly referring to his first wife, Elizabeth Weber, who had travelled to LA with him and worked at the Executive Room behind the bar. And then there was the businessman getting stoned, sharing a lonely drink with all the other characters who had been expertly brought together by Billy's storytelling.

How can you not be enchanted by a story like that? Everyone can relate to at least one of those characters. Who hasn't felt lonely in a crowd, sharing a drink? And the music. A timeless, waltzing, classical piece interspersed with the harmonica that segues the song together. This song has come to epitomise Billy Joel, and is now reserved for the finale at every gig. Back in 1984, at the time of this concert, Billy appeared to have no real concept of quite how popular this song was, remarking to himself at the conclusion of the song and appearing to write himself a note: "Crowd likes Piano Man". He always looks a bit awkward with the ill-fitting harmonica brace around his neck, singing, playing the piano and the harmonica all at the same time. But now it is a sing-along anthem, popular with Billy's mature audience who perhaps all recall being businessmen slowly getting stoned when they were younger.

In fact, this song inspired me so much, I went out and bought a harmonica – one of those cheap £2 ones in a blue box, and have mastered the "in/out" sound (clearly demonstrating here the extent of my technical musical knowledge), reproducing it perfectly (or so I thought) as I play the album on my stereo at home.

Three songs follow in quick succession: *Don't Ask Me Why* – which talks about every drunk getting their drink, perhaps an acknowledgement of Billy's love of all things alcoholic at the time. And the great lyric which describes having to spend your life standing in line, but at the same time acknowledging that at least you're still standing on your feet. Perhaps this is an acceptance that we all have to do what we're told from time to time and how angry this can make you feel, so regardless of what happens, life carries on.

Then *Allentown* – a stonking great tune which brilliantly tells the story of a typical industrialised East Coast American town suffering the economic downturn of early eighties America, particularly in the steel industry. It could have been written by Springsteen in the same vein as *Born In The USA*, songs which, on the face of it, seem to be about everything that is great about America, but listen to the words, and it's the polar opposite.

The good folk of Allentown weren't too pleased with this at first. But they asked Billy to donate a percentage of his royalties to the town to set up a scholarship, and rewarded him with the key to the City. He might be angry, but he's clearly a great guy.

Next, and from the same album, was *Goodnight Saigon*. A song about the Vietnam War. Oddly, not a protest song as you might expect, but a story told through the eyes of a young marine about the fear and camaraderie of war. For this tune the road crew are called in to contribute to the chorus complete with the sound of chirping crickets and menacing helicopters, combined with roving "search lights" across the stage, the song comes alive. God Bless America.

Just then Billy runs across the stage, up a ramp and stands behind a synthesizer and before we know it, we're getting the opening chords of *Pressure*. If ever a song summed up my life at this time, this was it. I've just taken A levels – I need a job. I wanna be a rock star – I've got no talent. I want a girlfriend – there's no chance. PRESSURE. ARGHHH. PRESSURE.

That's it. I'm not just angry anymore. I'm about to fucking explode with rage. Look at Billy's face. He's singing this like he means it. PRESSURE. PRESSURE. ARGHH. PRESSURE. He's singing this for me, because he understands me. What a song. I need to calm the fuck down or I'm gonna punch someone.

The song comes to an end and the gig takes a swerve as Billy indulges in some of his "new" material from *An Innocent Man. Leave A Tender Moment Alone*, with guest harmonica player, the late Toots Thielemans, followed by the title track of the album.

I too, was an Innocent Man. Misunderstood, left in the dark. I'd sing this song alone, at the top of my voice in my bedroom. Reaching for the high notes. Not knowing if I'd made it. Here at Wembley, standing high in the bleachers, I was singing again – at the top of my voice – to the horror of those around me. Boy. This is a tough song to sing. But I think I just nailed it. Bam. I am An Innocent Fan.

The Longest Time was up next, acapella style. Not my favourite song. It's not angry enough for me. This is a song about someone finding love. Bloody hell. We can't all date Christie Brinkley, you know. This was followed by *This Night*. And more about that song later.

Then the music takes us back to 1977, and *Just The Way You Are*. The quintessential Billy Joel love song. Covered hundreds of times, this song is a legend in its own right. It nearly never made it onto The Stranger album, but eventually went on to become Joel's first US Top 10 hit. Written for his first wife Elizabeth, Joel and his band allegedly never really liked the song. It won a Grammy. It was not without controversy, as some thought the lyrics were demeaning to women and portrayed them just as objects to be desired, rather than listened to. It didn't matter to me. I love this song. And if I ever get a girlfriend, this will be the song we dance to at our wedding.

And then we're back at the piano, for the unmistakeable opening chords of *Scenes From An Italian Restaurant*. A massive "ahhhh" goes up from the crowd in Wembley.

This was the song that turned me on to Billy Joel. It was 1978 when I first heard it and my sister had just bought The Stranger album. She'd sit and listen to it in her bedroom, and if I was lucky, I could sit on the end of her bed and listen too. As an imaginative young boy, aged 12, hearing the story of Brenda and Eddie as they meet for a nostalgic drink to reminisce about their past, broken relationship simply enchanted me. And then the song transports us back in time to when Brenda and Eddie were the coolest couple in Hicksville. I just pictured this young couple in the 1950s, Eddie with greased back hair, and Brenda with her fifties dress on. Hanging out at the Village Green (more about that later, too). Driving around in their 1950's convertible, with the radio on. Getting married, and then two years later it all falls apart. In concert we hear the line about waving the couple goodbye with Billy sat at the piano, waving at the crowd as they wave back. And then the song transports us back to the present day.

Never released as a single, and more than seven minutes long, this song is right up there with Piano Man as a Billy Joel standard. It was the song that changed my life and led to me buying every record Billy Joel had ever made, desperate to hear more stories like this.

From the moment I heard that song, I vowed to visit **that** Italian restaurant, find out who Brenda and Eddie were and hang out at the Village Green. More about that later.

This concert was getting too much for me. The frustration of being sat "in the Gods" surrounded by people who, I thought, didn't deserve to be there, I needed to get closer to the action. But how?

The stewards at Wembley were a pretty well organised bunch. It's generally impossible to switch sections at these arena gigs, probably for good reason, but I didn't care. I'd paid good money to be at this concert, and I wanted my money's worth.

In terms of the playlist, things were being ramped up a notch or two with *Sometimes A Fantasy*. An odd little rocker about phone sex. Yes. Phone sex. Banned by some radio stations because of the risqué lyrics and implications, it featured on the *Glass Houses* album.

I hatched a plan. I could see the stewards had removed the barrier from the front of the stage, and people were up and dancing. I needed to get down there fast.

"Sorry. Excuse me. Need to get by", I said to the non-believers sat around me. I made my way briefly out of the arena, up to the bar and ordered TWO pints of beer, served in plastic "wobble" glasses.

I then made my way DOWNSTAIRS and onto the arena floor, slopping beer along the way and – now this is the key bit – with my ticket in my mouth.

The concert was in full flow, everyone on the arena floor was stood by their seats. It was pretty chaotic. I made it past the first check point, waving two pints of beer in the air, and gesturing to the stewards to take the ticket out my mouth if they wanted to check the seat and block number. I was waved through. And the same as I entered Block B on the arena floor, and then straight past the last checkpoint, beer slopping down my arms and dribble from my mouth. No-one was gonna challenge me now. To those dumb stewards it simply appeared I was returning to my non-existent girlfriend with a drink after being sent to the bar. Genius.

And there I was. I couldn't believe it. I'd made it to the front. I simply put the drinks, which I didn't even want, on the floor and was at the front of the stage, resting my elbows on that sacred platform. This was no Fantasy, I'd actually made it. For a moment, my anger had changed to euphoria.

With the opening chords of *It's Still Rock n Roll To Me* blaring out in the arena, here I was, within smelling distance of my mentor, my brother, my inspiration and he was singing *It's Still Rock N Roll To Me* TO ME!

I love this song. Of course I know all the words. All my friends were into New Wave at this stage of the eighties (I pretended I was) and this song stuck two fingers up to them, declaring whatever the genre, it's still rock n roll to me.

I'm singing at the top of my voice, asking what the matter was with the crowd I was seeing, knowing that the lyrics referred to my own situation, and knowing they were so out of touch. Right now I was hip. I was trendy.

I was at the front of this concert. I was resting on the stage. In my mind, I was ON the stage.

I'm singing the final verse at the top of my voice and just then, Billy swings the mike out to the crowd, straight at ME and I get to sing INTO HIS MIKE the final line of this great, classic song.

Just for that moment, I heard myself through those massive Wembley speakers, shouting, completely tuneless to 11,999 non-fans that it's still rock n roll to me. And it was.

Could my life get any better? Billy had been scanning the crowd as he sang the song, scouting someone out who knew the words and was singing along, and that person was me. We'd connected. For a moment, both our DNA was on that mike. I'm a rock star. I'm an angry rock star. I'm a *Big Shot*!

And what a great song that is. According to Billy, *Big Shot* was written after he'd had dinner with Mick and Bianca Jagger, but in another interview some time later, he claimed the song referred to himself and his own ego.

But the crowd are loving it. Billy's on top of the piano, spinning around, going wild. I know we're in encore territory here and I'm right. We finish off with two huge rockers: *You Maybe Right* and finally *Only The Good Die Young*. And if that's true, I'm gonna live forever.

And this was the start of my Billy Joel journey. What a concert. It was as though I'd been on stage with the entire band. And I wanted more.

CHAPTER TWO
TELL YOU ABOUT IT

And so I set out to find out what I could about Billy Joel. Sure, I knew most of the better known songs – most people do. But I wanted to meet other people like me. People who had become so touched, affected even, by his words and music, that it had changed their life.

And so 32 years after sitting at that concert, and singing that line, my journey really began.

Over those intervening years, I'd spent hundreds. No. Thousands of my British Sterling Pounds buying all of Billy's singles, albums and cassettes and then buying them all over again during the CD revolution. I'd been to almost 20 concerts in the UK and even the US. Purchased "remastered" editions, "anniversary" editions, "special" editions, "bootleg" editions. Scoured second hand shops and markets for "collectible" editions, and with the birth of the internet, "world-wide-web" editions.

But for me, it was always about the live show. Because it didn't matter if he was singing *Just The Way You Are*, or *Uptown Girl*, the expression on his face looked like he wanted to smash your fucking teeth in.

From Wembley Arena to Las Vegas, Connecticut to the Hammersmith Odeon, or Madison Square Garden to Wembley Stadium, I've been there - and got the t-shirt.

With advancing years, I needed to understand more about the man who created the music for the soundtrack of My Life.

And so I arranged the first of many trips to New York, and more specifically Long Island. And more specifically than that, Hicksville. Where it all began.

Let me make this clear. This is not a Billy Joel biography. I never set out to write Billy's biography. There are already a couple of versions out there. And I don't claim to be an absolute authority on all things Billy. But I am a fan. And so this book is written by a fan, for the fans, with contributions from fans along the way.

In addition to this, I've tracked down and spoken to some pretty cool people. People in his current band; his former bands and others who in some way have had their own lives affected in one way or another by either the man himself or his music.

In the pages and chapters that follow, you will read about all the various people we met and interviewed along the way, from London to New York, Florida, California and Las Vegas.

When read together, you'll get a unique picture of Billy Joel. Different to anything you will have ever read about Billy Joel before.

I acknowledge that, annoyingly, this book flits from UK English, to American English, but it was just proving impossible to be consistent with names etc. Sorry about that!

CHAPTER THREE
THE HASSLES

Before Billy Joel, there was The Hassles, Long Island's most popular band.

They didn't know it at the time, but the band was to be the launch platform for an unknown teenager who was to become an American icon.

But more than that, original members of The Hassles were to play a lifelong and life changing part in Billy's young life and ultimately introduce him to a woman who was to become the inspiration for some of the greatest love songs ever written. I'll say that again. Ever. Written.

Unlike subsequent musicians, life-long friendships were to be forged, but also the ultimate betrayal between best friends.

The role The Hassles played in creating the Billy Joel we know today cannot be understated, and I needed to talk to the one person who was there, who witnessed these crazy psychedelic days, who kept the peace between friends, original Hassles guitarist Richard McKenna.

Formed in 1965, the original line-up consisted of John Dizek on lead vocals, Jon Small on drums, organist Harry Weber with Richard on guitar.

Even before Billy was a part of the band, The Hassles had a residency at a club in Plainview, Long Island called My House. Managed by the enigmatic Danny Mazur, The Hassles had hordes of teenagers lining up around the block every night, in much the same way The Beatles did when they played The Cavern in Liverpool.

I managed to track Richard down to his home in Florida and persuade him to talk about those heady days 53 years ago when four guys from New York looked set to challenge four guys from Liverpool in their search for worldwide domination.

The Beatles and The Hassles seemed to have a lot in common during those early days, including a time when the band almost stole the show at The Beatles 1966 appearance at Shea Stadium.

Richard picks up the story: "We were good friends with the manager of The Young Rascals and he made a proposal for us to crash the Beatles concert at Shea Stadium.

"It would have been the biggest thing that ever happened. We actually got our equipment on stage. I remember The Ronettes were on the show, another band, then us and then The Beatles."

Sadly, due to timings, the plan didn't come off: "We were in their dressing room and I did get to meet Ringo, Paul and John, but not George. Ringo actually asked me for a light. He was very nice.

"We were in the dug-out when The Beatles came from their dressing room to go on stage. Incredible," recalls Richard.

This was during a time before Billy joined the band, and it wasn't going to be long before Richard experienced Hasslemania for himself.

"We had a full sound for a four piece band," said Richard. "John Dizek was the front man, the Mick Jagger type guy of the band. We did a lot of cover music and not a lot of writing in those days. You would have to play music that was popular at the time, The Beatles, The Rolling Stones.

"As the times changed a little bit, we started developing our own sound and writing our own material. Danny Mazur was the owner of the club and he really loved the band and wanted to manage us. He had connections with people in the record business."

The band spent six months auditioning for various record labels. "United Artists really liked us and they offered us a five year contract from 1966 to 1971, which was provisional," said Richard.

"You had to do a single with an A side and a B side and if that record showed promise and got into the Hot 100 Billboard – which it did, they'd keep you on the label. *You Got Me Hummin'* was the name of the song."

Just as the band were teetering on the edge of breaking into the big time, organist Harry Weber was taking the band in a direction they couldn't afford to go, for risk of blowing the record deal.

"Harry ran into some legal trouble which was putting our contract in danger. He was arrested a few times and things like that. He had bad habits to do with drugs," recalled Richard.

"He was an excellent musician and singer, and his younger sister Elizabeth was married to Jon Small, our drummer, but there was a vote taken by members of the band that we had to find someone new."

And so the search was underway to find a replacement for Harry Weber. And with a flourishing Long Island music scene The Hassles, weren't short of choice. But they wanted the best they could get.

"There were lots of other bands playing at the time, but there was one particular band called The Lost Souls, and they had an extraordinary keyboard player who had an extraordinarily unique voice."

And that incredible artist was a 17 year old Billy Joel.

"We had three weeks of auditioning, and he was like the seventeenth keyboard player we had seen and he did a cover version of The Four Seasons song, *Sherry* and we finally picked him. Billy was thrilled about it.

"He was just about to turn 18, and he basically dropped out of school and the next thing we know we're in the studio for a month recording an album – the first Hassles album, and it was quite a good album.

"It included a song written by Steve Winwood (and Jim Capaldi and Chris Wood) called *Coloured Rain* and Billy sang that. Billy didn't sing every lead, because John was the lead singer. I was the lead guitarist and sang harmonies."

Having been welcomed into the band, Billy suggested they take on his close friend and Lost Souls bass player Howie Blauvelt.

"He was an excellent bass player and he actually broadened our sound live and gave us a fuller sound, so we became a five piece," said Richard.

One thing they all agreed on, was that new recruit Billy Joel was talented way beyond his years: "The unique thing about recording with Billy in the studio was that for such a young guy he could sing on a 'dry' microphone without any effects and never go off pitch.

"At the time he had a five octave range, almost like Michael Jackson. He could sing very very high notes and it blended well with the band."

And so The Hassles first album, called simply The Hassles, was gaining traction, supported by gigs, shows and even television appearances.

"In those days if you were on a label from Long Island or New York, it was hard to broaden your fan base, so were going to Massachusetts, Florida and up and down the East Coast and the Midwest. They liked our sound up there.

"We didn't hit the West Coast because in 1967 and 1968 they were into the West Coast Sound which was very psychedelic like Jefferson Airplane, Grateful Dead and The Doors and it was a different sound that we had. We were a very danceable band with a very good drummer, Jon Small. He was excellent."

And so prior to joining The Hassles, a teenage Billy had been largely restricted to High School or church gigs and now found himself signed to a major label as part of the biggest band on Long Island.

But it was back at The Hassles' spiritual home, My House, that a real buzz was building, and while the World was reeling from Beatlemania, Long Island was seeing Hasslemania.

"It was kind of Hasslemania in the making," said Richard. "The club held 400 – 500 people, so it was a pretty big club."

And for the first time in their lives, all the talent and the hard work was starting to pay off. The financial rewards were starting to come through.

"We would play at Danny's club, but he wasn't paying us the kind of money we could get if we went out on the road. We were making like $200 a night to play in his club, meanwhile he was charging $4/5 on the door to get in per person and it had a capacity of about 500, so he was doing very well."

Born and raised in Queens, New York, Richard moved to Syosset, Long Island with his family when he was just 13, and he could never have imagined the direction his life was now taking.

"I was with The Hassles from the age of 19 – 24, five years, and for at least three of those years we were recording and touring. We went from a bar band to a prestigious club band and because we were signed to a top label, we could be playing clubs in New York City five nights a week.

"At one point in 1968, we were getting $5,000 a night to do two shows of 45 minute sets. That was good money".

But only a fraction of that made its way to the band: "If I saw $500 out of that by the time you were done with everything, I was lucky.

"It was a lot of money in those days. But booking agents were taking 10 – 15% off the top, we had our contract with Mazur, and he got 20% of everything we made and then the record company would take their promotional costs out of the royalties, and believe me, they kept track of everything.

"I think Frank Sinatra once said, if you're in the entertainment business, you have to expect to give away 50 – 60% of your earnings, and it's really true.

"But we were doing a lot of shows. One time we opened for James Brown and it just blew me away because the people liked us – it was an outdoor raceway and there were 10,000 people there. Just to be part of that was unique."

It was around this time, on another occasion, that Billy Joel potentially saved the life of a young Stevie Wonder: "We were playing with Stevie Wonder in Central Park one summer time. Stevie was 18 or 19 at the time and they called him 'Little Stevie Wonder'.

"He was on stage playing harmonica, jumping around with his band, and he got very close to the end of the stage and it looked like he was going to lose his balance and fall off.

"The first person to notice this was Billy and he grabbed him by his shirt and managed to pull him back on stage just in time. That was a fond memory," says Richard.

Touring with Billy was always exciting: "It was a lot of fun," says Richard. "Billy was a natural comedian and he could imitate other people like Walter Cronkite or John Wayne. He has a natural ability at picking up other people's voices, and often when he sang, people said he sounded like Paul McCartney. His voice sounds very similar.

"A lot of times we were on stage doing a Wilson Pickett song like In *The Midnight Hour*, and he sounded just like Wilson Pickett if he wanted to. He had this natural ability to sound like others. I think it was a gifted quality that he had. That and his musicianship on the piano."

"We did six to seven hundred shows together. We had a very good live sound and when we played live, it was exciting. We were a heavy duty band.

We were very tight on stage.

"That's the way they wanted you do play in those days. They wanted you to play it exactly the way you did in the studio."

But by the time the second album was released, Hour Of The Wolf, things were starting to change: "This was more of a heavier duty, kind of drug orientated and influenced album. It was very good, but it didn't really have a great direction. It didn't have a specific song on the album that really caught people's attention.

"Although there was a song called *Country Boy*, which was a very good rocking song. Then after that we did a single called *Travellin' Band*, followed by a rock version of the Jerry Lee Lewis song called *Great Balls Of Fire*.

By now, things were starting to slow down for The Hassles. People's taste in music was changing with the times, and by 1969, the screaming fans had gone, and Hasslemania was a thing of the past.

With the band falling apart, members started to go their separate ways. However, Billy clung on to drummer Jon Small and together formed the psychedelic heavy rock duet, Attila.

Billy moved in with Jon, his wife Elizabeth and their young son. But while musically Jon and Billy were struggling to recapture the magic of The Hassles, a chemistry of a different kind was developing between Billy and Elizabeth – his best friend's wife.

"It's very hard for me to discuss this," says Richard. "I don't want to put anyone down or say anything bad.

"Personally I don't know how Billy ended up with Elizabeth. I can't say who fell in love with who, but she wound up with Billy and went off to California with him at that point," added Richard, unwilling to discuss the matter further.

But what isn't in dispute is, during Billy's early days with Elizabeth, she was the influence for some of the greatest songs ever written; *She's Got A Way*; *Just The Way You Are*; *Everybody Loves You Now*; *Always A Woman To Me* etc etc. Elizabeth went on to become Billy's manager and first wife.

"We did our thing with The Hassles, and it ran its course," says a matter of fact Richard. "I really respect Billy and give him a lot of credit.

Because of Billy's continued popularity, Hassles material has been re-issued: "Billy doesn't even make any money from that," said Richard.

"Of course, I might have been a little bit jealous, but I realise what my limitations are. As a singer, I'm an average singer. He has a naturally pitched, gifted voice. And I believe that.

"There are times of, I wouldn't say jealousy, but I would say 'how come he didn't pick me to stay with him?', stuff like that. But for whatever reason, he made the changes and you're only as good as the band you have behind you."

And while Billy Joel went onto become, well, Billy Joel, Richard moved to sunnier climes and took up a career with the Postal Service, right up until the time he retired. But he never gave up his music, and continued to play in various bands, mostly on the wedding circuit.

"I'm happy Billy is so popular. If it wasn't for his popularity today, The Hassles would have gone down as one hit wonders, and a lot of groups would not be remembered. His popularity has meant our band has gone down in history as part of his career.

"He doesn't speak down of the band, and I compliment him for that. This was the beginning of his career and every now and then when he does a concert, he'll play a Hassles number.

"Billy developed his own style, but while he was with us, he was part of a band. A member of The Hassles," said Richard, almost bursting with pride.

Brushing over Billy's Cold Spring Harbor album, and the achievements made by his original touring band, Richard continues: "Billy went out on his own, and it took him three or four years before he really hit it.

"When Billy finally got his sound together with his original Billy Joel Band, and I'm talking about Liberty DeVitto, Richie Cannata, Doug Stegmeyer – God rest his soul - and Russell Javors, that's how he developed.

"Some things happened with Liberty and the band. I know what happened with Doug Stegmeyer and that was very sad. It was after he came back from the Russian tour and Billy just told him he wanted to get a different bass player. He had been with him from the start and that was very hard. He got into a big depression after Billy let him go" said Richard.

With shows selling out at Madison Square Garden on a monthly basis, and other shows throughout the States and around the world, what does Richard think of this continued success?

"People are paying $300 - $400 a ticket to see people, icons like Paul McCartney, Eric Clapton or Billy Joel. That's a lot of money to pay and hear the same material," says Richard.

"The last time I saw Billy in concert was in Miami about 10 years ago. I got back stage and we talked. He was not as joyous, happy and free as he is today.

"He had gone through another divorce and seemed to be doing the show because he loved to play on stage, but he didn't seem to have his whole heart into it at that point," recalls Richard.

With Billy's continued touring, does Richard think the surviving Hassles members will ever perform together again?: "A lot of people have asked me that," said Richard. "I would be okay with something like that happening, but it would have to be a part of something with Billy's band, because I'm not sure if Jon Small plays the drums anymore."

But if the live show doesn't happen, Richard, Billy and Jon could still be reunited if a campaign to get The Hassles inducted into the Long Island Music Hall of Fame continues to gain momentum.

"I was in touch with Elizabeth about two years ago and she was heavily involved in trying to get this to happen," said Richard.

How would he react today if he saw his former band member?: "I would say 'Hey Billy, how you doing? What's up man', shake his hand and give him a hug."

And so it might be almost 55 years ago, but Richard recalls with clarity, fondness and admiration the part he played in recognising the genius that is the Billy Joel we all know and love today. And he is counting down the days when they can one day play together again.

CHAPTER FOUR

BOTTLE OF RED? BOTTLE OF WHITE?

It's well documented that Billy's earlier songs were pretty autobiographical; drawing on his own life experiences, particularly where he grew up in Long Island.

So you don't have to be much of a Google stalker to find out where THE Italian Restaurant, made famous by the album track *Scenes From An Italian Restaurant,* was located. Now, there has been much debate about this. A similar debate rages amongst Beatles fans' as to the original location of the front door of The Cavern in Liverpool. It really doesn't matter *too* much. For me it's more about the romance of the song and walking in Billy's childhood/ teenage footsteps.

So, that quick Google search throws up Christiano's in the Long Island village of Syosset.

I first visited the restaurant in 2008, and returned again a year later in 2009, this time with my wife-to-be.

What a difference a year makes; hassle free flights to JFK and a free upgraded hire car meant we were seated at a table for two in by 6pm. Just perfect.

Now, those of you familiar with the song, will recognise the line about getting a table near the street, and those of you have visited Christiano's will know this isn't strictly accurate.

Christiano's is/was an unassuming restaurant in a parade of shops probably built in the early sixties with all the imagination of a prison block. Dull concrete exterior fronted by a parking lot. You wouldn't *want* a table near the street at this location.

Having visited once before, I knew what to expect and so was able to warn the soon-to-be Mrs B.

I had, however, asked for Billy's table, a booth toward the rear of the restaurant, and I was assured by staff this was his table of choice whenever he visited.

And, according to staff, it wasn't beyond the realms of possibility that he could "…call in at anytime". If he did, we'd all be sharing his favourite booth because there was NO WAY we were budging.

Inside the restaurant it is/was all dark wood, green carpets and red leather. There was a bar with a few stools against it and the owner mixing Martinis. There were only two or three other people dining, and I suspected there was no need to book. As you walk/walked into the restaurant there is a framed black and white photo of Billy circa 1973 (unsigned – which was disappointing) and a framed, yellowing newspaper cutting of an interview with Billy which appears to confirm Christiano's was, indeed, THE Italian Restaurant.

As mentioned previously, there has been much debate about this. Billy Joel admits that he was going for applause when he said onstage once that the Italian restaurant in "*Scenes From an Italian Restaurant*" was Christiano's in Syosset. "It was like saying 'Yankees' when you're playing in New York," he said, adding that it *was* a restaurant he frequented back in the day. He says there are two restaurants which provided inspiration for "*Italian Restaurant*" both of which are or were actually in Manhattan - Il Cortile in Little Italy and Fontana Di Trevi in Midtown.

But none of this mattered. I was there with Mrs B-to-be and we were, as far as I was concerned, sat in HIS favourite booth at THE Italian Restaurant.

The waitress came to take our order. The temptation to order a *"Bottle of red. Bottle of white"* was almost overwhelming, however, we decided to order a glass of red and a glass of white to maintain the authenticity of this magical moment. And it was magical.

The waitress delivered our order; I had the steak, Sharon the lasagne.

"I guess you get a lot of Billy Joel fans here, right?" I asked the waitress who had shown little in terms of customer service to this point. "A few," she said making no eye contact and sounding completely uninterested. "So", I persisted, "when was Billy last here?" "Oh, about a month ago I guess." I nearly fell off my/his seat. I sat up and immediately turned my gaze to the door expecting him to walk in any moment now, a visit being long overdue.

"What was he like", I asked like a wide-eyed schoolboy. "Katie (his wife at the time) is lovely". Not quite the answer I was expecting. "But what was *he* like?" I asked again. "Well," said the waitress, he ordered dinner like he usually does, ate it, and left." "Okay", I thought. "And that's it?" I asked probing for something a little more in way of detail. "Oh" she added. "He didn't pay. He never pays whenever he comes here. It's kind of understood. He didn't leave a tip either." "Really?" I asked. "Free dinner and no tip?" surely she was mistaken. "Nope. They upped and left. A few moments later Katie returned and left something on the table. Like I said, Katie is lovely".

Now, I'd heard Billy has a reputation for being a bit grumpy on occasion, but tight? Surely this can't be true. I have no-way of verifying this story, and it could be staff at Christiano's are/were sick and tired of Billy fans ordering bottles of red, white or whatever and asking stupid Billy Joel related questions, but this wasn't what I was expecting to hear.

We returned to the location in 2018, this time with a local resident who was able to tell us the story behind one of the most famous and popular restaurants on Long Island. You can read about that later in the book.

Sadly, Christiano's is now a Chinese restaurant with a new name. I thought Billy would have bought it. But he didn't.

CHAPTER FIVE

LARRY RUSSELL – PART ONE. I WAS THE FIRST.

Larry Russell's story has never been told…until now.

The original bass player – actually the original member - of the Billy Joel Band, says he has never received the recognition or reward he deserves, despite touring and performing in what has been widely accepted as some of Billy Joel's most important live shows of his career.

Some conspiracy theorists say Larry Russell has been deliberately "airbrushed" out of Billy Joel's history; his pivotal role in Billy's early success cruelly overlooked or, even worse, dismissed.

After much persuasion and negotiation, with many emails and messages flying across the Atlantic between us, Larry agreed to meet me and talk about the ill-fated Cold Spring Harbor Tour of 1971-72.

We had arranged to meet Larry, a resident of Manhattan, but originally from The Bronx, at the City Diner in the Upper West Side, Larry's local eatery of choice and the only place he would feel comfortable recalling long since buried memories of a time long, long ago, but not forgotten.

Larry's story is emotional. His feelings toward Billy Joel as bittersweet as any Billy Joel love song. Full of love, with twisted ironies and an undercurrent of hatred. The best example of that contorted love/pain/hatred and love again is the track Stiletto from the album 52nd Street. Listen to it.

As he recalls the events of a tour which launched Billy's career, and should have changed Larry's life, the love and respect he has for Billy as a performer is clear to see. But the contempt he feels toward the same person for not, as Larry says, "doing the right thing" is also there, but somehow always softened by a sigh or faltering of the voice.

Larry first encountered Billy in 1967 when he was drumming in his band Age Of Reason, "It was the most exciting time," recalled Larry, "things were starting to happen and no-one knew how to handle it.

"We auditioned for a guy called Danny Mazur who owned a club called My House which was in a shopping mall in Plainview, Long Island. We had a record deal at the time with United Artists."

Billy was playing for resident My House band, The Hassles. "We opened for The Hassles," said Larry, "and that was the beginning of our relationship. Billy was great. Billy was tremendous. His talent was obvious. The whole band were great, but he was the most talented out of the bunch".

And so with a flourishing Long Island music scene, Larry and Billy's paths would often cross, but they never had the opportunity to play together.

That was until a chance meeting when Larry literally ran into Billy's manager Irwin Mazur (son of My House owner, Danny) in New York City in September 1971.

"I literally ran into Irwin in the street. I asked how he was and how Billy was doing. He told me Billy was making a new solo record and was looking for a band. I told him I'm playing bass now and did he need a bass player. He said 'we need everything!', so at that point they didn't have anybody. I was the first in the band," said Larry.

Irwin arranged for Larry to listen to the recording of Cold Spring Harbor and to learn the songs prior to auditioning: "It was just the two of us at the audition, and the first thing Billy says to me was 'Oh. You look older'. It had been a while since I had seen Billy and I had a moustache in those days," said Larry, who was 21 years old at the time, and a year younger than Joel.

"So I picked up the bass and we went through the songs. There was just the piano. There was no drummer. There was nobody else. It was just the two of us and that was it. Eventually, Irwin said to me 'You're in'".

A rehearsal schedule was arranged at a recording studio in Long Island and auditions planned to recruit other band members. And this was the beginning of the financial pain for Larry Russell.

"I was there every day," said Larry. "I had to travel from The Bronx where I lived to Manhattan, and then out to Long Island by train. I didn't get paid. I wasn't reimbursed for my expenses. Nothing. Nobody offered. You didn't think about it back then, but I think about it now. Why didn't they reimburse me?

"I was there for everyday that we rehearsed or auditioned. I thought it was fantastic, because here we are rehearsing in a recording studio and I thought 'Wow. They have money. This is gonna go'.

"We auditioned a lot of guitar players and we got Al (Hertzberg). He seemed like he wasn't really into it, but saw it as an opportunity.

"None of the drummers seemed right for Billy, so the Suits got in Rhys Clark because he was the only one that was going to make us sound like the record. He showed up and it was just perfect. We gelled the way the record gelled. We weren't getting paid a dime at this stage."

As rehearsals continued, Larry and Billy's friendship deepened and Billy would start to confide in Larry, revealing a vulnerable side during his song writing process.

"Billy started introducing new songs, like Travellin' Prayer. He would look up at me and say 'Larry, shall we do this?' He didn't always know what was working and whether it was good enough. He knew how to write them, but he didn't know if they were great.

"And I would look at him and say 'No no no. You gotta do this…' I think part of me liked it because we were adding our parts. And then I remember when he wrote Captain Jack. He didn't have the whole thing. He started off with the F chord which was the verse, but before that, the intro that he does now, starts off with the chorus riff.

"I was very vocal about what I liked and what I didn't like. I felt that we were friends and that we were doing things together here. I have a producer's head. I always have."

Larry recalls an occasion at the Media Sound studio on 57th Street while work on Captain Jack and other songs was continuing. "We were going over some songs, and I said to Billy "Can I talk to you?" and he said 'What's up?' I said 'Can we fix that line (on Captain Jack) because it was a bit herky jerky.

"He had something progressive sounding like Yes and it didn't work. He said 'What do you mean? Like this?' and I said 'Yes. That's better'.

"But do I ever get any recognition for that? Does he ever say I want to thank you Larry or I want to thank these guys who were there? No. I just wanted it to be right. I wanted it to sound good just like he did. I didn't write the part, I just urged him to change what he had. That's what you do when you're in a band with Billy. He doesn't know it all."

Produced by the enigmatic Artie Ripp, the album Cold Spring Harbor contains many memorable tracks – all catastrophically recorded too fast, famously making Billy sound like a chipmonk.

While other record companies and major labels were choosing to pass on Billy, Artie saw something in the kid that others hadn't seen, or were unwilling to invest in.

Famously shrewd, Artie Ripp became rich beyond his wildest dreams by persuading an eager and inexperienced Billy to sign a water-tight contract that even the mighty Columbia Records had to take a hit on before they could release him from it.

But Larry Russell was there in those early days, and has a different take on a part of Billy's history that Billy – and certainly Billy's accountant, would rather forget.

"Billy used to put Artie Ripp down too much," said Larry. "He wasn't much of a producer and he made one fatal error speeding up Cold Spring Harbor and not noticing. That was bad.

"But Artie was the only one who put $50,000 of 1971 money into Billy's career when no-one else would. Everyone else had turned him down. And to not recognise that is ungrateful, in my opinion. I think Artie got 25 cents a record. So what? He had to make his investment back".

With the band fully rehearsed, they relocated to Los Angeles at the start of January 1972. It was widely recognised back then that LA was the place to be and to be seen.

Artie and Irwin worked hard getting the unknown Billy Joel and his band gigs. But there was just one place to get noticed in those days, The Troubadour. Located on Santa Monica Boulevard in West Hollywood, in the early seventies, this legendary venue was breaking stars like Neil Diamond, Elton John and James Taylor. The list of names is endless.

"We played The Troubadour a bunch of times," recalled Larry. "In those days you'd play a venue for maybe four or five nights. A lot of people made their name there. We were getting paid something like $30 a week at this point. That's like $4 a day.

"I don't remember how they got jobs for us, because they had to support us to keep making money," says Larry.

But while the money was nowhere to be seen – and Billy was in the same boat as the rest of the band, the gigs were coming thick and fast, mostly on the college circuit with a view to Billy building a live following.

Artie and Irwin secured shows all over the country, plus some major gigs including opening for the Beach Boys at the Miami Convention Centre.

But it was a controversial Puerto Rican festival which was to prove a game changer for Billy; The Mar Y Sol festival which was to catapult Billy to the attention of record company execs back on the West Coast:

The Mar Y Sol – meaning Sea And Sun, Pop Festival took place over three days at the beginning of April 1972 – Easter Weekend. For the deeply religious Puerto Ricans, the idea of a Woodstock-style sex, drugs and rock n roll weekend bender did not sit comfortably with the authorities.

There were some big hitters on the bill: Alice Cooper, BB King, Black Sabbath, Fleetwood Mac, Rod Stewart and the Faces to name but a few. But the festival was dogged with scandal, including two drownings and even a murder. The weekend was labelled by critics as "unsuccessful" and "uncomfortable", all except for one artist.

"I remember getting into the helicopter and flying into the festival ground," says Larry. "I felt like I was flying into Vietnam or something. Billy and Rhys were sitting behind me and I had my bass between my legs and there was no door. And then we saw the showground. Thirty thousand people. This was a really big gig.

"And I was getting nervous because I was worried Billy's material was not going to be rockin' enough for these people. I wasn't sure She's Got A Way would be the kind of music people wanted to hear.

"We landed and the roadies showed us to these shacks made of bamboo and we're hanging around for a while before it's time to go on."

In 1972, health and safety didn't feature too highly on most rock promoters' list of things to think of, and when the rain started to fall on Day 2 of the festival, things started getting dangerous.

"And so we go on and do our set – and I got electrocuted. I was stunned," said Larry. "So the roadies pulled out some plastic sheeting from somewhere for me to stand on so I could carry on playing my bass. Just crazy!"

Playing to a field full of tents, music fans were at first reluctant to come out of their shelter as the rain poured. But curiosity started to get the better of people, and by the time The Ballad Of Billy The Kid and Captain Jack was played, faces started popping out everywhere.

"And then we do our first encore, and Billy does his Joe Cocker impersonation. It was so real and the crowd were going crazy. We left the stage and went to the dressing room, smoked a joint – I turned Billy onto grass on that tour - and then Irwin runs in and says 'Larry. We're on stage again'. And we went up and we did Jumpin' Jack Flash and then finally Billy introduced the band. First names only though.

"I look back at that and think it could have been any Larry. Any Rhys. Any Al. But they didn't know us. 'I'm Billy Joel if you didn't catch my name'. That's what he said.

"This was a massive success for Billy, because we knew it was the first time we were able to control that many people."

And while the festival itself, which was dogged by bad weather and crime, was a disaster for many of the top names on the bill, one name stood out: Billy Joel.

Recognised by many as Billy Joel's first major gig, the New York Times who reviewed the festival said: "The first real excitement was generated by Billy Joel's gospel-tinged rock band who brought some life to what had been a generally dispirited environment".

"This gig was so special," says Larry now, looking back almost 50 years. "Something like this had never happened before, and it surprised him, that he was able to do that. Prior to this we had played colleges of around two to three thousand people. This was special."

CHAPTER SIX

LARRY RUSSELL - PART TWO. THE SIGMA STUDIO SESSIONS

Still riding high on the success of the festival-stealing Mar Y Sol show, greater things were just around the corner for Billy, but Larry and Al would be heading home...broke.

So while the gigs and the crowds were getting bigger, this somehow wasn't being reflected in the pay checks.

"We weren't making money," says Larry. "It was always 'OK. The money will come'. But it never did. That's what I'm bitter about."

But the buzz around Billy Joel was building. And at Philadelphia's WMMR radio station, they got it. Despite its misgivings, the radio station got the vibe from the Cold Spring Harbor album, and on the back of the Mar Y Sol success, offered Billy a prime time Sigma Studios session with DJ Ed Sciaky.

This was a gig way ahead of its time: Recorded in front of a live audience, and broadcast simultaneously, it was to prove the ultimate showcase for Billy Joel.

"It was right after Mar Y Sol," explained Larry Russell. "We had a feeling of bravado. We felt we could take on anything. And that's why the Sigma recording sounds so good. I still love it. It was a beautiful memory. Wonderful".

Larry takes a moment and looks away, reflecting on this memory. Clearly proud of the achievements made on a tour that made no money, but what was to make a superstar out of Billy Joel.

The Sigma Studios set list was impressive. And listening to the banter of a young, but confident Billy Joel between tracks revealed a little more about this Long Island wise guy.

Tracks included *Travellin' Prayer, She's Got A Way, Everybody Loves You Now* and *The Ballad of Billy The Kid*. But the stand-out track was *Captain Jack*. A song that captured the imagination of a dispirited American youth. A story about drugs and masturbation and a song considered by many to be the most important of Billy's early career.

Larry says: "Maybe that one song stood out because of the word 'masturbate'. In those days it seemed a bit unruly in a way to say that, but that's mild by today's standards!"

The repeated airplay of this one track brought Billy, but not the rest of the band, to the attention once again of the major record labels, and the Big Time was just around the corner.

But for Larry and Al, the money had finally run out. The band split and went their separate ways, with Billy dismissing the entire tour as a disaster. No-one, it seemed, had made money from this outing. Only drummer Rhys Clark would remain with Billy.

"We had great times on the road," says Larry. "I kept Billy laughing a lot. We enjoyed the fun things. Yes, he was the boss, but I could speak freely around Billy because I knew him. I wasn't afraid of him and I respected him. There's a part of me that loves Billy, because I know how he can be, but it annoyed the shit out of me when on the Sigma recording he introduced me as 'On the bass. It's Larry Larue from The Bronx'. It felt so disrespectful.

"We were in an office with him in Los Angeles, and I remember knowing this was the end. We were going to be sent home. There were no more gigs until further notice. I was homeless. I had no place to live.

"I called Billy into a room on our own, and I said to him 'I just want to tell you that it was a privilege doing this tour and having this experience with you', and he was like 'Yeah. I know'.

"There was no feeling, and I felt like going 'HELLO. IT'S ME. Say something'. My God that hurt me. There was nothing there but bullshit. I looked at him and thought 'this man has no clue what I'm talking about'. It's all about him.

"He's a narcissist. During the rehearsal days back in Long Island, we would hang out at the park and at one point he just came out and said: 'I'M GONNA BE A STAR'. I looked at him and just thought 'wow'. So that's what this is about, and it irked me."

But Billy's prophecy was to become true. And while his star was getting ready to shine, Billy and Larry went their separate ways.

1972 was a sobering year for Larry. Returning to New York City, he realised that his Billy Joel days were behind him, and he had to pick up the pieces of his own life and find a way of bringing in the dollars, something that never happened with Billy.

But it didn't take long for things to turn around, and Larry spent the next few years touring the country with the likes of The Mamas and the Pappas, Mary Travers and Gary US Bonds. Between 1973 and 1976 he toured with the show Godspell.

And this was to be Larry's life for the seventies, eighties, nineties and beyond; performing, touring, producing and developing new and exciting musical concepts including movie soundtracks and working with other artists. Life was good for Larry Russell.

But he never forgot his friend, Billy Joel. He never stopped thinking about those early days of playing endless gigs, helping to build the reputation and legacy of a future American Icon, and being paid pennies.

"I wrote to Billy. I wrote him a lot," Larry Russell says to me as we're sat in the City Diner in October 2018.

"I wrote to him on the road. I had a career on Broadway. Billy came to see me on the road and I would always write to him and send him a postcard.

"I'm talking about when I was in LA doing Godspell. I went to visit him at his house there. Everytime I went to see him and I had not seen him in a while, he would be so excited to see me."

"The song *Souvenir*? I believe he wrote that for me. Because when I first heard it: A picture postcard. A folded stub. A programme from the play. He came to see me in Godspell. In '73 he wasn't going to plays. He had no money. He didn't have clothing. He'd wear the same clothes for years.

"And that song came out, and I said to myself 'Ahhh. That sounds familiar'. But it's not a good song. In it he's saying 'file away'. I really feel that's true and I was hurt."

But with the passing of time, those meetings would become less frequent.

"When *The Stranger* came out, I heard there was to be a party and I went to it. I felt I belonged there. And Billy was okay with me. He came up to me and after introducing me to Liberty DeVitto said 'I was so angry with you for so long', and I realised why he said that.

"I remember writing to him and saying 'By the way Billy. You're song *Roberta* sounds a lot like *Forget Him* by Bobby Rydell'. It is exactly the same song melodically. I asked him why he was so mad with me. He got really close to me – because we were friends, and he said 'You're the only one that knew that'.

The letters would continue. In 1985 Larry sent Billy a note congratulating him on the birth of his first daughter, Alexa Ray.

But in 1992, Larry wasn't feeling so pleased for his old friend: "I'm watching the TV and I heard 'Billy Joel has just contributed $50,000 to a school for a flooded piano'. And it just hurt me. I thought 'Are you kidding me?'

"So I wrote him another note. Not nasty, but correct. I said 'Look. None of us (Larry, Rhys and Al) is doing great. It's true. So, you know Billy. We were there for you. It's time for you to be there for us'.

"Well. He called me. This was July 1992. It was the weirdest day. I answered the phone. He asked 'Is this Larry?' I said 'Yeah. Who's this?' He said 'Billy Joel'.

"He sounded so stern and matter of fact. But it was not nice too. You can be matter of fact and still nice too. He said 'Larry. Do you have a lawyer?' I laughed and said 'It's not about that'. I was clear. Well, he denied we were on the road together. He denied it was a tour. He said it was a "radio hop".

"It was more than that. He should have paid for everything in terms of what the result was.

"So Billy was denying this, denying that. Then the minute he found out I didn't have a lawyer, he softened up. I said to him 'Billy. You SOUND like a lawyer'. Where's the love? It didn't exist. It was his choice. He could have said anything to me.

"Then he tried to soften, and he said 'Well, you know, we should have dinner together'. He always said that. He never does though.

"I go back and forth. I love hate love hate him. I don't hate him. I am just disappointed by him. Disappointed by his behaviour, because a lot of time has gone by where he had time to think about it and he chose not to.

"I wrote him again after that and said 'So when do you want to have dinner?' Somehow I got to him. Billy loves me. It seems deep down inside he does. But he can't let go of a penny".

But it took Larry and Billy's mutual friend, Jeff Schock, to point out to Larry it was bad timing, and the early 90's weren't a good time for Billy financially having discovered he had no money himself and had been ripped off by former managers.

"I said to Jeff I know that now, but when is the timing ever good? When is the time okay to talk about that? When is the time to remember your legacy, Billy? What about us? We either need recognition, which he'll never give us, or money, or both. Why not both? He can afford it. Give us $100,000 each. Why not? Are you gonna miss that money? Or a percentage of something? I've had 50 years of being annoyed. It's too much."

Larry looks away again. I ask him if he's okay to continue, or does he want to take a moment? "This is therapy," he says. "I need it every now and then".

He continues: "I can understand him changing the band. That's fine. I'm not annoyed about that."

Then turning his thoughts to another of Billy's bass players, Doug Stegmeyer: Why do you think he killed himself? He was hurt. Did he give him money? Did he give him severance pay? Well, that's what you should do. With me, Billy probably thinks 'Oh well. He's got my name to go on'".

CHAPTER SEVEN

BALLAD OF BILLY THE PUNK

Visitors to New York are unlikely to visit Long Island. Motels and accommodation closer to the main Borough's are sparse and uninviting, and the further east you go, completely unaffordable.

Most definitely commuter belt territory, the historic Long Island Railroad links these communities to Penn Station in Downtown Manhattan – right underneath Madison Square Garden, the spiritual home of Billy Joel whose record breaking residency at the legendary venue is unsurpassed.

For this trip, the September 2009 visit, we based ourselves at the Hicksville Econo Lodge. Heading east on the 495, we decide to leave the highway and opt for a leisurely two hour drive through some of the prettiest (and most expensive) neighbourhoods in New York State, known as The Hamptons. We soon arrive in the millionaire's playground of Sag Harbor. Strange name to us Brits, this former whaling community is now THE place for the rich and famous.

I'd never heard of Sag Harbor until 2007. I watched a programme on UK television called The South Bank Show. Presented by Melvyn Bragg (also a strange name to us Brits, and you Americans too, I guess), this "arts" programme broadcast late on Sunday evenings, usually focused on high-brow "artsy-fartsy" bollocks that didn't interest me at all (sorry Melvyn). But when I saw it was to feature an interview with Billy, I had to watch it.

2007 was just starting to see a resurgence in Billy's popularity. Billy and the fans had come to accept that Billy wouldn't be writing any new material, and he was happy (commercially, anyway) to rest on his quite remarkable laurels and let the hits do the talking.

The Bragg interview is one of the best available to see. Billy looks relaxed, and Melvyn asks the kind of questions that many a fan has pondered over for decades: "Why is Movin' Out subtitled Anthony's Song?" for example. What makes this interview special is that it's not filmed in front of a live audience, with all the whooping and hollering so common on American talk shows. This was about Billy and the music.

The interview is out there for all to see, so it would be pointless repeating chunks of it here. What interested me about this unique piece of TV history, is that it revealed the location of the one-to-one chat was Billy's Sag Harbor home. "SHARON. We're going to Sag Harbor".

Now. Finding affordable accommodation in Sag Harbor isn't easy, and we settled for a room at the Sag Harbor Motel (which I believe has since been renamed). At approximately $300 a night, it was the nearest thing to an Econo Lodge you're gonna find in these parts.

On high Billy alert, we strolled up and down the quaint High Street lapping up the September sunshine, stopping to visit the antique shops and gift shops along the way. We shared a tuna sandwich in a Sag Harbor deli which cost a fortune and was bloody awful (surprising for American food), but it allowed us to use the toilet (or bathroom as you Americans might say). We stopped by one gift shop and I got chatting to the young assistant. Intrigued by my accent, she asked where we were from.

"We're from London," I said. "Oh wow. That's so cool", confirming my theory that not many Brits take the time to visit Long Island. "What brings you here?" she asked. And before I had the chance to answer, from the other side of the store, Sharon volunteered "Billy Joel". I did cringe a little, preferring to keep the purpose of our visit a little closer to my chest, and feeling a little unsure about how the locals would react.

"Do you guys even know who he is?" asked the clerk. "I mean, we think of Billy as one of our own. We see him in the street – he's always hanging out downtown, riding his bikes or walking his dogs. We don't see him as this famous rock guy. That's so cool".

Did I hear this right? Always hanging around downtown. Walking dogs. Riding bikes. "SHARON. Get the camera!"

We headed over to the Sag Harbor Diner. Two strawberry milkshakes and a seat in the window. Nope. No sign of Billy.

We hit the street again, window shopping before spotting a small gift shop selling shells and shell related ornaments. Just off the main drag up an alley, the store had a few crooked steps leading up to a small creaking door. Everything inside was quirky and unique. As the sun shone through the window it cast a dusty shadow.

As we browsed the eclectic collection, I noticed the clerk in the corner, slim and with long hair. She was leaning over a laptop, glasses perched on the end of her nose. She barely noticed we were in the store until Sharon approached the till to buy a bracelet.

Realising we weren't local, she asked the inevitable question: "What brings you guys to Sag Harbor then?" As before, with no time to answer, Sharon butted in: "He loves Billy Joel. We're here to find Billy".

"FUCK OFF" she quite literally screamed, causing me to jump. Not quite what I was expecting. She snatched the glasses from the end of her nose and just when I was expecting to be told to leave her shop and never return, she added: "That's so FUCKING cool", emphasising the "F" bomb. "You guys have come all this way to see Bill?" "Bill?" Does she know him? "You know he has a house here, right?" she asks. "Well", I said in a very quiet and British kind of way, "I thought maybe he did".

"It's just around the corner. YOU'VE GOTTA CHECK IT OUT. Look for the house with the buoys all over it, just opposite the harbour and next to the Legion Club. YOU CAN'T FUCKING MISS IT.

"If you're really lucky and he's home, the barn doors will be open and you'll hear him playing. If he's in town, he's always in The Legion, drinking or eating. I think his boat's in the harbour. I know the skipper."

And so, we quite literally walked around the corner and there it was; Billy's converted boathouse, right on the sidewalk and overlooking the harbour. As we walked past, we peered in through the storm shutters and saw his collection of classic motorbikes and juke boxes which were just visible.

We bought an ice cream and found a bench nearby with views of the upstairs terrace which appeared to be laid out as if for lunch, and the front door. But there was no music playing, and quite clearly no-one in.

After six hours of sitting there (I'm just kidding. That's a joke.) After half an hour of sitting there, I could sense Sharon was getting a little bored. We decided to book a table for dinner at The Legion that evening and headed back to the shell shop.

"Not there?" asks the clerk. "That sucks. Let me tell you where his beach house is. Maybe he's there."

Is this crazy woman for real? Is she sending us on a wild goose chase, laughing behind our backs?

Armed with directions, and the good advice of "when you get to the sea, stop driving," we set off in search of his beach house. Like his Sag Harbor home, the beach "house" (colonial mansion is a better description) is easily accessible from the beach and a public footpath which passes between two neighbouring properties.

We're out the car. Sharon is wearing a pair of bright blue dungarees purchased the day before, and she has strict instructions to photograph anything that moves. As we run up and down between the two properties, photographing the one on the right, it's clear there's no-one home, while I spot workmen working on the neighbouring property on the left elbowing each other and laughing at our antics.

We return to the shell shop, where Debbie-Lou (we're on first name terms by now), helpfully Googles Billy Joel's beach properties only to reveal that, at the time of our visit, he recently purchased BOTH properties, the one on the left most recently from movie star Roy Schneider which was being re-modelled to Billy's liking. Was he there? We'll never know. We concentrated on the other house and he definitely wasn't in that one!

But we'd made a new friend. Debbie-Lou seemed to take an instant liking to Sharon and I, and I got the distinct feeling she'd be less willing to help out the more "fanatical" fans, which was fine by me. We're still in touch with her today.

Dinner at the Legion was a tasty, but uneventful evening. Strategically sat with a visual containment on all doors and exits. If Billy had ANY ideas at all of popping in for dinner or a drink tonight, I was gonna know about it. He didn't. But the food was good.

The following morning and our time at Sag Harbor had come to an end. With one last drive past the Boathouse and The Legion Club (just in case), we headed north to the Long Island community of Rocky Point, pop. 13,597.

Driving through town, there doesn't seem to be much, er, point to Rocky Point. No downtown area that I could see, just a pretty dull street with not much happening. Long Island's North shore at this point seemed to lack a certain charm found further East. But there was a reason why we're here in Rocky Point, and it's something I'm very excited about. We were visiting a church.

There are a few artists who perform the music of Billy Joel well. Not as some cheap tribute act, but as serious musical aficionados of the man and his songbook.

One of those is Mike DelGuidice. A Long Island musician of some repute who made a name for himself with his tribute act called Big Shot. You'll learn much more about Mike and his amazing career later in this book.

Long Island has a close knit musical community, and word soon spread about Mike to Tommy Byrnes, who is Billy's lead guitarist. He'd heard that "this guy DelGuidice is pretty cool".

So, on down days and when he's not touring, Tommy hooked up with Mike, and other distinguished Long Island musicians to lift Big Shot to the Big Time, so much so, that during one Long Island gig, Billy himself turned up and joined the band on stage. Imagine that. Billy Joel playing in a Billy Joel tribute band. That's just insane.

But, in a moment that rock n roll dreams are made of, Mike was asked to join the Billy Joel band. For real.

And so now, in-between gigs, Mike's Big Shot featuring Tommy Byrnes, Billy's drummer Chuck Burgi and other Billy related musicians reproduce the magic.

Full details of this amazing tale are told later, by both Mike and Tommy who speak exclusively about life on the road with Billy Joel.

And it just so happened, that Big Shot were putting on a free outdoor gig in the church carpark (that's a parking lot for my American readers) in Rocky Point. Hence the reason for the drive from Sag Harbor. Well, there was a chance Billy could rock up at Rocky Point? Who knew?

Arriving early, we quickly found the church car park and saw the stage was to be an open-sided articulated lorry. I don't think Billy is likely to show up for this particular gig.

With a bit of time to spare, we searched for somewhere for dinner. There was definitely an exciting atmosphere building in Rocky Point and the local Police were beginning to shut the road immediately outside the church, clearly anticipating a large crowd.

Over the road, I spotted Deks, which describes itself as an American Restaurant and Taproom. We had no idea what a Taproom was, but it didn't matter because we were hungry and the place was filling up. Rapidly.

Ordering a starter of French Onion Soup for Mrs B and chicken wings for me, by now they were queuing out the door for a table. And the kitchen was clearly struggling to cope. Starters done, we waited for the main course. And waited. And waited. A guy who clearly looked like the owner was looking flustered and was perspiring while dealing with unhappy diners.

I called him over. A large man wearing a tight blue t-shirt revealing an ample belly and shorts, probably aged early 60's. "You must be Dek?" I asked. "I'm the 'D' from Deks," he said as he explained the name was made up of the initials of the three joint owners.

"You're busy here tonight," I said. "Yep" was the response. Surprisingly 'D' didn't appear to pick up on the English accent. "I guess they're all here for the free show," I said, hoping for some meaningful conversation while we waited for our burgers. "Yeah. Guess so," he said. "Billy Joel tribute show," I offered. "Maybe. Whatever" was his response. Now this response really threw me. Because everyone else I'd spoken to on Long Island puffed their chests out with pride at the mere mention of Billy Joel, Long Island's most famous export.

What he said next nearly made me fall off my chair. Making no eye contact, and raising his voice considerably, and not caring who might be listening, D boomed: "The guy's a two bit punk. He's not welcome in my restaurant. I don't care who the fuck he thinks he is."

I didn't know what to do. Should I get up and walk out in protest? I definitely decided in THAT moment I at least wouldn't be leaving a tip. Maybe that's why Billy wasn't welcome there because he hadn't left a tip. After all, he appears to have previous for that. But we were hungry, so we stayed put. Protest over. I have principles but, well, when you're hungry, you're hungry, right?

"Why do you feel like that?" I asked, slightly frightened to hear the answer. Turning his considerable bulk to face me, and narrowing his eyes, D leaned in toward me and said: "My older brother went to school with that punk. He thought he was some big shot, even then.

"He ran with The Parkway Green boys. Bad boys. Punks. They had it in for my brother and beat the shit outta him all over some broad."

I couldn't believe what I was hearing. But certainly what he was describing rang true. D's age and approximate age of his brother. The gangs. The Village Green. The troublesome youth mixing with the wrong crowd. Engineer boots, leather jackets and tight blue jeans. Okay, I made the last bit up.

"Billy Joel?" I asked seeking confirmation we were taking about the same person. "Yeah. Like I said. The guy's a punk. I don't know who threw the punches, but as far as I was concerned, he was part of it."

And with that, our burgers were thrown down in front of us and D stomped off muttering under his breath. "Punk".

Of course, I can't verify any of this is true. And I don't really care. However, the encounter as described here is true. Maybe the details have become a little fuzzy over the years, but a great story, nevertheless.

CHAPTER EIGHT
RHYS CLARK – BILLY WAS MY BEST MAN

Lots of people around the world choose a Billy Joel tune for their wedding dance, but not many can say: "Billy Joel was my Best Man".

Drummer Rhys Clark can.

But then Rhys has a very special and unique connection with Billy dating back to the early seventies that, despite heartbreak along the way, has led to an endearing lifetime friendship. I had to find out more.

Hailing from New Zealand, Rhys started drumming as a teenager and in the sixties was one of the founding members of top Australian band The Executives who between 1966 – 1969 had a number of hits, and even their own TV special.

In 1969, The Executives recorded an album in the United States. This was to be their last and the band split up shortly afterwards. Some members returned to Australia, but Rhys stayed in the US to follow his rock n roll dream and he became one of LA's most sought after session drummers.

It was while he was in Los Angeles that Rhys hooked up with controversial music impresario Artie Ripp. The same Artie Ripp that famously signed Billy to his own label in a water tight deal that still sees Artie make a royalty to this day.

Speaking to me from his Huntington Beach home in Orange County, Rhys picks up the story: "It's 1971 and Artie signed Billy from The Hassles and brought him and Irwin Mazur to LA to do an album. I was picked by Artie to join him and we had our first meeting.

"I had heard seven songs that he had demoed and I can remember a wonderful apprehension about our first meeting. He had excellent material that was challenging for me."

And so together with bass guitarist Larry Russell and guitarist Al Hertzberg, the first Billy Joel touring band was born.

But what was unusual about Rhys was that his friendship with Billy was to go beyond the ill-fated Cold Spring Harbor album and tour.

Everyone knew the production of Billy's solo debut had been screwed up, but people were trying to remain positive. Rhys says: "I'll try and be diplomatic about it, but it was part of a bunch of things that were negative. The mixes were not very good, but we were all new to this, and it was like taking a gamble.

"It was the Piano Man tour that was the beginning of his rise," explained Rhys. "With Billy it felt like I was on board his ship and it was picking up speed and I had been given the opportunity to come along for the ride.

"Being with Billy on this journey was awe-inspiring. We were opening in venues one day and very quickly returning to the same place as the headline act. This was huge," said Rhys with an obvious sense of pride.

Rhys had been on the road with Billy and his first wife Elizabeth from 1971, and witnessed the intensity of their relationship as his own friendship with Billy deepened and a trust developed.

And so Billy was thrilled when Rhys asked him to be the Best Man at his wedding to wife Marilyn. Elizabeth was maid-of-honour. This created a bond which was to last to this present day.

Rhys understood more than most the pressure Billy was under to produce new material for what was to become Piano Man – he witnessed it for himself.

Rhys was with Billy beyond the 1974 release of his third studio album, Streetlife Serenade, and the associated tour that went with it which stretched into 1975, but he didn't actually appear on the album itself.

"I was disappointed that I didn't get the opportunity to do a track on the Streetlife album," says Rhys, "but Billy was under a lot of pressure and he had to produce new songs. He had to make every note count. Our pressure was just to support him and watch him grow as an artist."

But the good days came to an abrupt end at the conclusion of the Streetlife Serenade tour. "Billy invited Marilyn and I over for dinner. He knew I was from New Zealand and they had made roast lamb." But it was then that Billy dropped the bombshell: "They told us they were headed back to New York."

Stunned by the news, Rhys recalls it being an unusual dinner party, with Billy and Elizabeth asking Rhys if he wanted to buy their LA home.

"Within two weeks, they were gone. It broke my heart that I knew this wasn't going to continue. But I got over it. I know the cruel nature of this business. I was pleased I got to play with Billy when I did. I'm very grateful for my experience and my life with him.

"There were no ill-feelings and there is no stain on our relationship. I didn't hurt him and he didn't hurt me. We maintained a gracious relationship. It's part of business and part of life.

"I don't share Larry (Russell's) feelings at all. It's just how it goes. Billy doesn't have to respond to that. He has got to keep it moving because that's what he wants to do.

"I tend to shy away from Larry and his attitude at being disappointed with Billy because it serves no good purpose. I might feel some resentment, but I'm a more positive person and lean toward the more positive nature of it all."

Rhys looks back on the Cold Spring Harbor tour, and remembers the highlights of being there at the birth of an American icon.

"It was exciting times and each place we played was a wonderful and unique challenge. We were the underdogs, but we were out to rock the place," said Rhys.

There were two stand out highlights from the tour, he says, the Puerto Rican Mar Y Sol festival, and the Sigma radio sessions in Philadelphia.

"Billy ended up being the act that blew them away at Mar Y Sol," recalls Rhys. "A typical late afternoon tropical downpour turned Billy's 35 minute performance into an hour.

"His time slot was dead in the middle of the festival. The circumstances just went his way, and that downpour fuelled his performance. By the time he did the Joe Cocker number, the crowds surged forward, because they thought it was Joe Cocker on stage!"

Rhys was 25 at the time of the festival and he remembers it being a drug fuelled, and frightening experience.

"There was talk that someone had been stabbed, another person raped and people getting ripped off. The Puerto Ricans didn't want us there and they were trying to tear down the fences."

Despite the controversy, Billy's performance was a great success, receiving rave reviews that helped bolster a loss making tour.

Soon after returning to The States, the band were lined up for the Sigma radio sessions, a live broadcast in front of a small audience. "It turned out pretty good," says Rhys. "But we were all nervous.

"The nervousness was part of the pressure, but because of Billy's tower of talent, he was able to handle it and use it to his advantage."

But as 1975 came to a close, Rhys found himself looking for new projects, and, indirectly, it was Billy and Artie Ripp who were there to support him.

"I talked with Artie Ripp just a few years ago," says Rhys, "and my status on Artie is that he appreciated what I did. And I thanked him for that.

"I respect him and he put me together with Billy. And he looked after me after that work fragmented and ground to a halt. It was a great ride."

Between 1979 – 1999, Rhys toured with American folk singer/songwriter Hoyt Axton and contributed to the success of dozens of other artists.

But when Larry Russell approached Rhys to be a part of the Sigma reunion shows in 2013, he said he was thrilled to be playing with his old band mates, but never for a moment believed Billy would show up to be a part of it.

"I love the trouble that Larry went to to put those shows together and to have the opportunity to recreate my part in those songs together with Don Evans.

"I also now have an infinite appreciation of Elio Pace and David Clark who stepped into the role filling Billy's shoes. Elio's enthusiasm was incredible and Elio is now a part of my life in the same respectful way that Billy is," says Rhys.

It was during the 2013 Sigma reunion shows in New York that Rhys had the opportunity to catch up with Billy himself: "We got together at his motorcycle shop and Marilyn and I met him and Brian Ruggles (Billy's long-time sound engineer) for lunch. It was a wonderful experience."

And Billy never forgot his old friend. As recently as 2017, Billy once again reached out the hand of friendship to Rhys: "In January of 2017, Billy's archivist Jeff Schock called me on some archives he had questions about. During the conversation he said to me 'by the way, can you check your calendar and see if you have May 13 open'.

"The reason was that Billy was coming to play the LA Dodger Stadium and he was going to do a selection from his song list that reflected his time in Los Angeles."

Naturally the show was a sell-out. But as Rhys watched the show from the side of the stage, he wasn't prepared for what happened next. With emotion in his voice, he said: "Billy introduced me on stage to 53,000 people. Emotionally it was incredible and I felt like my mom and dad were smiling down over that stadium at me.

"Billy was giving me a moment. My moment. I got some applause, but no-one knew me. Billy turned and whispered to me: 'I'm glad you're here'. I'll never forget it."

And a review of the gig by the Los Angeles Times acknowledged: "The Long Island native waxed nostalgically about the years he spent in LA in the early days of his career.

"He reminisced about toiling at the piano bar and romped through his Ronettes/Phil Spector pastiche, *Say Goodbye To Hollywood*."

Does 72 year old Rhys think there will be an opportunity to play with Billy again?: "Larry (Russell) keeps saying we should open for Billy at Madison Square Garden, but the favour would be too big. I explained to Larry we can't do that. It's not right."

Nowadays Rhys just plays for pleasure, preferring to spend time with Marilyn, his wife of 46 years. But I get the sense that he will never tire of transporting himself back to those days in the early 70's and talking about the time when he was there at the musical birth of an American legend.

> *"We went to his shop today and he was there with his mechanics. The shop was closed. He saw us looking in and he opened the door. He said come on in and he was so nice and we took pictures with him."* **Ralph Perna Jr**, **TX**.

CHAPTER NINE

SAY HELLO TO HICKSVILLE - SEPTEMBER 2009

It becomes apparent quite quickly that Hicksville, Long Island, Billy's childhood home, is not exactly top of New York States tourist destinations.

In fact, a quick search on Hotels.com gives a choice of just two motels; a Day's Inn and an Econo Lodge. You're unlikely to take a relaxing spa break at either of these locations.

But this was no holiday. There would be no time for *massages in garages* (Billy lyric of sorts there for the eagle eyed readers amongst you), this was a rock 'n roll tour with the purpose of discovering the inspiration for many of Billy's hits.

Having made the relatively short journey from Christiano's to Hicksville, we settled into the Econo Lodge, maps at the ready for tomorrow's trip back to the 50's and the streets where Billy grew up.

Many books and countless articles have already chronicled the Joels' journey which eventually brought them to the post-war Levittown development of Hicksville. His father's somewhat nomadic lifestyle which saw his work taking him travelling for much of the time, leaving the young Billy and his sister Judith in the care of mother Rosalind.

When Billy's father Howard, eventually left the family home to return to Vienna, turning his back on his young family, it meant Rosalind was left to raise the children and Billy becoming the man of the house.

Even though times were tough, Rosalind recognised that the young Billy had inherited his father's musical abilities and sent Billy for piano lessons, not quite realising how talented her son actually was. Billy has often discussed his ability to play by ear, make up classical sounding tunes and pass them off as the work of some of the great composers of times gone by.

But growing up in a neighbourhood like Hicksville, and Mommy paying for your piano lessons, led to problems of their own for Billy who found himself mocked and bullied by other kids in the neighbourhood. So, in addition to pounding the piano keyboard, Billy took up boxing and was a force to be reckoned with and was soon left alone by the other kids.

Desperate to fit in, Billy found himself hanging out with the wrong kind of crowd – the Parkway Green Gang. A street punk, smoking, wearing a leather jacket and skipping school. Could this be the "Eddie" we've heard about?

Driving around Hicksville is a little like stepping back in time. Our motel was close to the Long Island Railroad and the sounds of the trains added to the 1950s feel of this commuting community.

Like most things Billy Joel related, it's easy enough to find 20 Meeting Lane, Hicksville, Billy's childhood home. And what a surprise. Wide, tree lined streets, houses with cared for front gardens (or yards as our American cousins would say), and certainly not the run down slum you might expect of a housing development from the post-war era. Certainly similar developments in the UK have not fared so well or maintain any of the charm found here in suburban Hicksville.

I was in the driving seat for this particular trip with Mrs B in charge of satnavs, maps and, most importantly, camera.

This was no treasure hunt. There were no cryptic clues to follow. We had the address and before we knew it, we were conducting our very own slow motion "drive-by" trying to get the best shot we could. By the fourth attempt,

I was happy. Unlike the residents in the street who had probably seen this kind of behaviour a thousand times before and probably didn't care for the pollution.

The white wooden structure has changed slightly and been extended by various owners over the years, but it still maintains its own charm and it's easy to picture Billy climbing out his bedroom window late at night to hang out with the guys at the Parkway Green Gang at the Village Green, *Half A Mile Away*.

It didn't look like anyone was home. And there's no "blue plaque" marking the historic importance of this house. And don't under-estimate that historic importance. Billy's life and music has influenced many generations around the world and continues to do so.

Now, Mrs B isn't backward at coming forward when it comes to knocking on the front doors of stranger's houses. A good example of this was during another trip to Long Island and a visit to the coastal community of Amityville. The true story of the horrific murders at 112 Ocean Avenue in Amityville and the subsequent movies have made the town a macabre tourist destination.

To cut a fascinating story short, on this particular occasion, before you could say "That house is haunted", Mrs B had hoped out the hire car and was knocking on the door hoping the current owners would give us a tour. No-one was in, but a photo speaks a thousand words and the shot of Mrs B on the doorstep of 112 Ocean Avenue is still a talking point at many a dinner party for us.

Back to Meeting Lane, Hicksville, and I was getting the sense that the locals were getting a little fed up of me driving up and down at a snail's pace outside this suburban address, with one or two appearing to reach for their brooms and rakes. Fearing a lynching, and despite me wanting Mrs B to try the same brazen door-knocking I'd witnessed previously on Long Island, it felt like it was time to leave.

And so Sharon and Jonny did their best Brenda and Eddie impression and drove off *with the car top down and everyone waving Sharon and Jonny goodbye.* Okay. Give me a break!

A short drive around the corner is Hicksville High School where, famously, Billy Joel never graduated, telling teachers "I ain't going to Columbia University, I'm going to Columbia Records", or words to that effect.

A talented student, with a particular interest in history, Billy wasn't bothered about school. He was all about the music. Short in stature, and shy around the girls, Billy found his musical genius, even at a young age, was all he needed to impress and make him one of the cool guys.

To me, that era evokes images of the hit movie Grease. And looking around Hicksville High, it could easily be substituted for the fictional Rydell High where Danny (John Travolta) and Sandy (Olivia Newton John) had some *Summer Lovin'.*

A magical era of Americana. Rebellious youth, fumbling romantic encounters, rock n roll, glamorous cars and drive-in movies. What must it have been like growing up then and there? No mobile phones. No internet. Just leather jackets and tight blue jeans.

Not far from there we reach our final destination of our tour of Hicksville. The Village Green.

No signs to speak of. No acknowledgement of the musical importance of the location where Brenda and Eddie were hanging out.

A small space, surrounded by suburban roads and various other buildings, it's slightly harder to imagine Billy and his gang of street punks causing chaos.

Despite the rain, nothing was going to stop us hanging out at the village green. We parked up and, holding hands, stepped onto the grass. Arms out-stretched, clasping hands standing opposite each other, we looked up and closed our eyes as the rain gently fell on our faces. We allowed our thoughts to drift back to the early to mid-sixties; musically a pre-Beatles and post-Elvis era full of excitement and a feeling of anything's possible. The American Dream. And for just that moment, we were part of it.

Left: Billy's childhood home in Meeting Lane, Hicksville.

Photo: John Marchut.

Right: Welcome to Hicksville.

Below: Hanging out with John Marchut at the Village Green.

Photos: Sharon Brett

Right: Hicksville High School. Billy didn't graduate from there until 1992 – 25 years after leaving. He famously said: "If I'm not going to Columbia University, I'm going to Columbia Records." And he did.

Photo: Sharon Brett

Above: The Hassles. L-R: Billy Joel, Richard McKenna, Jon Small, John Dizek and Howie Blauvelt.

Photo supplied by: Richard McKenna

Above and left: Richard McKenna today.

Photo supplied by: Richard McKenna

Below: Village Green 2018 and laundromat where Billy would often find himself sleeping after a late gig before school.

Right: Larry Russell gets animated.

Photo: Sharon Brett

Above: Rhys Clark today

Below: Larry Russell

Above: On the road 1972 style. L-R: Mrs Mazur, Irwin Mazur, Annie, Elizabeth Weber, Larry Russell, Al Hertzberg and Billy.

Below right: Larry relaxes on the beach in Puerto Rico, 1972. Billy features top right corner!

Photos: Rhys Clark Collection

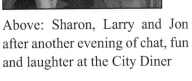

Above: Sharon, Larry and Jon after another evening of chat, fun and laughter at the City Diner

Left: Mike Stutz grabs a selfie with pal Michael DelGuidice.

Mike Stutz, founder of the Billy Joel Completely Retold Facebook group, Billy Joel genius and all round Good Guy.

Below: Mike strikes a familiar pose on THOSE steps.

Photos: Supplied by Mike Stutz

Bizarre By Piers Morgan

Re-written review of Billy's Storm Front gig, May 1990. Piers describes Billy as "...an orangutan with a spear in its back". Last part written by me.*Cutting reproduced with permission from News Licensing.

Left: Smudged Alexa Ray Joel autograph on the cover of her Sketches CD.

THE SUN, Wednesday, May 23, 1990   13

★★ caught live ★★★☆

An uptown time with rockin' Billy

BILLY JOEL has always struck me as a miserable old devil.

He is one of the richest men in pop, he's married to one of the most beautiful women in the world and sells millions of records.

But I've seen more happiness on the face of an orangutan with a spear in its back.

Shuffling on stage at Wembley Arena in his trendy shades, Billy looked a right misery but the show was slick, lively and good value.

Billy is a hugely talented man and he had the audience rocking from the start.

He played all his hits, including the classic Uptown Girl

Bizarre rating: An Uptown show Billy!

TOMMY BYRNES, October 2018

Photos: Sharon Brett

Brothers: Hanging out with the legendary Tommy Byrnes in New York City.

"....and then Billy says to me 'You're in the band!'" Michael DelGuidice tells me about the moment Billy Joel changed his life.

Photos: Sharon Brett

Mike DelGuidice and Big Shot perform a set of Billy Joel rarities at The Iridium, New York City, October 2018. Photo: Sharon Brett

Left: A gathering of Billys.

L-R: David Clark (Lords of 52nd St), Mike DelGuidice (Billy Joel band, Big Shot), Wade Preston (Movin' Out), Matthew Friedman (Movin' Out), Christian Macchio (Capt Jack Tribute Band).

Photo: Sharon Brett

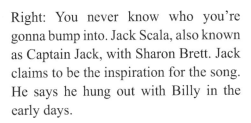

Right: You never know who you're gonna bump into. Jack Scala, also known as Captain Jack, with Sharon Brett. Jack claims to be the inspiration for the song. He says he hung out with Billy in the early days.

Photo: Jon Brett

CHAPTER TEN

MIKE STUTZ – COMPLETELY RETOLD

The internet's a wonderful thing. Particularly if you're under a certain age and know how to get the best out of it.

For Billy Joel fans around the world, the internet has brought everyone together to share a common love of the man and his music.

I first heard about the Billy Joel Completely Retold group during a trip to Sag Harbor, when we made friends with the eccentric Debbie-Lou who runs the sea shell store in town.

After chatting to her about Sag Harbor's most famous resident, and waving her hands around her ears, she said: "There's this whole weird internet community thing out there about him." When she said "weird", I don't think she meant it in a nasty sense, just an "amazed" sense that one person could be so globally popular.

You see, when Debbie-Lou in her Sag Harbor world thinks about Billy Joel, she thinks about the Long Island Boy who did "alright" and walks his Pugs around town from time to time ignoring everyone.

Founder of the Billy Joel Completely Retold group is a guy called Mike Stutz. Seven years ago he created the fan page on Facebook. It now boasts over 8,600 members from all over the world.

When I discovered the group, I must admit, I was more than a little bit annoyed. So much so, that I almost canned this book writing project. I wanted to be niche. I wanted to be the only person who "got" Billy Joel and his songs, and I wanted to be the person who spread the word about his greatness because I believed that even though MILLIONS of people have seen him in concert and played his music, they didn't *really* understand it. But then I got over myself.

Mike Stutz is an absolute authority on all things Billy, and he clearly has an "in" to members of the band and he regularly features selfies with the likes of Billy's guitarist Mike DelGuidice, and has even sung as a guest with Mike's band before.

There's no way I'd want to go one on one with Mike Stutz in a Billy bragging competition. He knows everything. However, I would challenge him to a Billy sing-off, because he's not the best singer! Check him out on You Tube if you don't believe me! (Just kidding Mike!)

A friendly, non-trolling group, people openly and enthusiastically share their thoughts and theories about everything Billy; from the meaning of the lyrics, to the clothes he wears on stage.

The group has even been known to put pressure on Billy and the band to include rare tracks and "deep cuts" to play lists ensuring the live shows are a little more than just Greatest Hits.

If ever Billy's "people" want to get a feeling of what the fans are thinking, I don't doubt for a minute that Mike Stutz would be their go-too person. Which is why it was so important for me to make contact with him and see if he would be willing to contribute to this project. Of course he would!

I managed to catch up with Mike over the Internet and find out exactly what turned him onto Billy. Here's what he told me:

"I can remember three distinct moments in the early Nineties that turned Billy into more than just a voice on the radio for me", said Mike.

"The first was in 10th grade, soon after Storm Front had been released. There was a girl I had a huge crush on, and one day I heard her walking down the hall quietly singing *And So It Goes* to herself. I was just starting to teach myself piano then, so I went and bought the sheet music book for Greatest Hits 1 & 2"

I guess we'll never find out what happened to the girl! Anyway, Mike continues: "A couple years later, I remember watching Billy's HBO Special *Live from Long Island*, where he ends with a short song I had never heard before called *Souvenir*.

"The lyrics just hit home with me, and it became my theme song - it was my Senior Yearbook quote, "Every Year's a Souvenir" became my sig phrase on web boards, and I even had a Geocities website called "Every Year's a Souvenir," said Mike. I ought to point out that I have little idea what Mike's talking about when he mentions "sig phrases and Geocities", which is probably why he launched an internet Facebook group about Billy Joel, and why I'm stuck in front of a typewriter writing about him. Pass the Tipp-Ex.

Anyway. Mike continues: "The third moment was at my very first Billy concert. It happened to be the same weekend as Woodstock '94 - the 30 Year Anniversary.

"Billy talked about how he had attended Woodstock, then did his spot-on imitation of Joe Cocker singing *With a Little Help from My Friends*. I spent the next 10 years trading tapes with fans on the Internet, searching for someone who had recorded that first concert of mine, until I finally found one."

I asked Mike what inspired him to set up the Retold Group some seven years ago, and why, exactly, did he decide to call it Billy Joel Completely Retold. Because it sounds a little weird to me: "Facebook had just recently started allowing the creation of "Groups" at that point.

"For the previous 15 years, I had been collecting and trading various Billy video clips with people on The Internet, and I thought it would be fun to start a group where I could easily share and chat about these videos with other fans from around the world.

"I had also been video-recording myself playing Billy songs on the piano, and a group seemed like a good way to share those with fans, as well."

But why call it Completely Retold?: "Back in college - around 1995 - the guy in the room next door to me was also a big Billy fan. One day, he gave me a cassette called "Billy Joel, Retold - Vol. 1." It was filled with studio demos of songs from The Bridge and 52nd Street albums - some had deleted verses, others had completely different arrangements.

"Several years later, I started a podcast where each episode would include different demos and the stories behind each song, which I named "Billy Joel: Completely Retold" as a tribute to that demo tape my college friend had given me. When it came time to name my fan page group on Facebook, it just sounded right."

So I'm guessing Mike would list some of Billy's earlier albums as his favourites. Right? Wrong!: "I have a special place in my heart for the *Greatest Hits 1&2* album, since it is was the first tape of his I purchased. I even modelled my High School Senior Photo after that album cover. Although, I must say that I listen to *Live From Long Island* more than any studio album."

The Retold Group is about to hit a remarkable milestone: "I take pride in how popular the group has become - at this time, we are currently approaching the 9000 member mark.

"As Admin, I've put in a lot of work over the years to find new content to share, and I've made a lot of new friends along the way. We even have previous band members as a part of our group!

"One of things I'm most proud of is how these guys who were with Billy back in the early 1970's are finally being praised in our group for their contributions to Billy's early music: Larry Russell, Rhys Clark, Don Evans - we even pitched in to get Al Herztberg his Platinum Record Award for his work on *Piano Man* - did you know artists have to pay for those awards themselves???"

So what does Mike feel sets Billy Joel apart from all the other singer/ songwriters out there? "I would say it's his ability to write songs in the styles of other artists, like a pastiche.

"You want a Robert Palmer-style song? He wrote *A Matter of Trust*. You want a Jimi Hendrix song? He wrote *Shameless*. Heck, he wrote the entire *Nylon Curtain* album in the style of The Beatles!

"Being able to take a popular style and write something to make it his own is a big part of what makes him unique, if that even makes sense.

"Have you ever heard his Joe Cocker impression??? The first concert of his I ever went to was the same weekend as Woodstock '94, and they sang *With a Little Help from My Friends*. You could have sworn Billy had left, and Joe had taken his place!"

Unlike most Billy Joel fans, Mike Stutz has a truly remarkable connection with Billy, and here he explains why: "In 1995, I got T-boned in my car by a pick-up doing 50mph. While I was in the hospital, my friends contacted Billy's people, and they got him to send a Get Well Package of CDs and swag.

"Four years later, when Billy was playing in Minneapolis, I was able to get backstage to thank him for helping me through some rough times. I gave him a big hug, and also gave him a pair of black sunglasses that he later pulled out onstage and wore for the song *New York State of Mind*."

Surely that must have been Mike's ONLY encounter with the Great Man?: "Other than meeting him backstage in 1999, I happened to meet him again by chance nearly two decades later.

"Last summer, as I stepped onto the grass at Target Field to get to our seats up front - a golf cart goes whizzing by with a familiar looking driver inconspicuously wearing a hat and sunglasses.

"When I saw the cart turning around, I put my phone into camera mode, and waited for the perfect moment to stop him and ask for a quick selfie."

Mike is fiercely protective of the Retold group and wants to encourage a feeling of "family" and "belonging" amongst members. But as with all families, there can be fall outs. And it can get ugly. Like, for example, if someone wants to compare The Lords of 52nd Street which features former members of Billy's 70's/80's touring group – drummer Liberty DeVitto, saxophonist Richie Cannata and guitarist Russell Javors, or Big Shot which features (amongst others) current band members Mike DelGuidice and Tommy Byrnes.

"You see - its arguments like this that I try to keep out of the group, because the fans can get pretty passionate about either side, and feelings get hurt," explains Mike.

"Watching The Lords gives you the nostalgia of seeing the actual musicians who recorded the original albums - and seeing Liberty DeVitto play the drums takes me back to my high school days of watching him play the kit like a Beast!

"Mike and Big Shot are doing a fantastic job of passing Billy's music on to a new generation of fans - plus, he let me get onstage at The Iridium earlier this year to sing one of my favourite Billy rarities *"Weekend Song."* But what I like is that BOTH groups help strengthen Billy's legacy."

Is Billy even aware this group exists? What would he think? "Yeah, he knows. His current guitar player, Mike DelGuidice is in our group, and he has told me he's shown Billy stuff from our group during rehearsals and such.

"He says Billy just has to laugh at some of the old stuff we've found where he was just goofing around in the studio.

"That's why I try so hard to keep Retold a respectable group, because you never know who's watching, right?"

How long does Mike think Billy can keep going?: "I just saw Billy perform his 100th show at Madison Square Garden last week, and I was literally standing front row, touching the stage.

"He says he'll do it until he loses the ability to do it well. He's 69 years old right now - and I thought he put on a fantastic show!!! So who knows how much longer we'll get the monthly shows - all I know is that, in our group, we look forward to each Residency Show, and have plenty of Retolders in attendance that the rest of us can live vicariously through them to feel like we are at every show!

"I would like to think that our group lives up to its name by giving fans a look behind the scenes of Billy's expansive career, and perhaps creating some new fans in the process!

"We've created mediafire and Youtube pages to store everything we've collected and make available to the public.

"I've filmed a series of Retold Location Videos where I visit Billy-related locations like the steps on the Innocent Man album cover or Billy's childhood neighbourhood to give fans a new perspective on his music.

"I've even created a sister page that I treat like a museum to archive rare and interesting photos that have been posted in the group. Anything to help preserve and strengthen the fandom for Billy's music," concludes Mike.

So. There you have it, ladies and gentlemen. An exclusive insight into the World Wide Web of Billy Joel fans, masterfully created by one superfan, for all to enjoy. Mike Stutz, we salute you.

THE SUN, Wednesday, May 23, 1990   13

★ ★ caught live ★ ★ ★

An uptown time with rockin' Billy

BILLY JOEL has always struck me as a miserable old devil.

He is one of the richest men in pop, he's married to one of the most beautiful woman in the world and sells millions of records.

But I've seen more happiness on the face of an orangutan with a spear in its back.

Shuffling on stage at Wembley Arena in his trendy shades, Billy looked a right misery but the show was slick, lively and good value.

Billy is a hugely talented man and he had the audience rocking from the start.

He played all his hits, including the classic Uptown Girl.

Bizarre rating: An Uptown show Billy!

CHAPTER ELEVEN

PIERS MORGAN (ALMOST) RUINED MY LIFE

Before he was an internationally renowned broadcaster, I'm rather proud to say that I spent some time working with Piers Morgan.

But that admiration became somewhat strained when, back in 1990, he described my rock idol as: "A miserable old devil with the face of an orangutan with a spear in its back". Which, I'm sure you'll agree, is harsh, to say the least.

So this is the tale: As a young reporter back in the late eighties, I started working at The Sun, Britain's most popular newspaper as a shift reporter, working mostly weekends and evenings.

Under the editorship of Kelvin MacKenzie, many would argue, myself included, that these were the real glory years of The Sun newspaper. Headlines like "GOTCHA" and "Freddie Starr Ate My Hamster" – which will mean nothing to my American readers – saw millions of copies of this paper sold each day.

It was Kelvin who recognised the talent of a young Piers Morgan and promoted him to showbiz editor. Piers had heard that I was keen to move from news reporting to showbiz, and so asked me to be a part of the team.

For me, getting the opportunity to work on the showbiz page, called Bizarre, at Britain's biggest paper was a pretty big deal.

My role largely consisted of running the Showbiz Desk on a Sunday, ensuring the column was ready for print on Monday. In addition to this I would put in regular evening and weekday shifts and supply exclusive showbiz news and stories at other times. This was a dream come true.

Even back then, Piers' talent as a tabloid journalist was recognised by publisher Rupert Murdoch who said of Piers: "His balls are bigger than his brain" or words to that effect, referring to Piers' willingness to take risks.

I was just proud to be working at The Sun. As a journalist, it's all I ever wanted to do. And so I was keen to impress Piers.

After spending many months building some top contacts with Columbia Records in London, I managed to secure a press pass for the hottest show in town – Billy Joel at Wembley Arena on Monday, May 21, 1990.

This was Billy's three year round the world Storm Front Tour, and to say tickets for his three London shows were like gold dust is an understatement.

I'd had to do some pretty serious negotiating with the Head of Press at Columbia to secure these passes, and they were expecting them to be put to good use. And a concert review in Britain's biggest selling newspaper swung it for me.

The show was awesome. Great Press seats with a superb view of the stage and some pre and post-show hospitability thrown in for good measure. Sadly there was no opportunity to meet Billy himself. Billy's dislike of the Press at this stage of his career was probably at its peak, and so the chance of sharing a sausage roll in his dressing room before the concert was never going to happen.

The set list featured all the hits, plus stand out tracks from the Storm Front album. Billy even included a couple of impromptu tunes; Rule Britannia and Shout, playing to his British audience.

I remember there being a real edge to this gig. The Storm Front album has some great rocking tracks on it, and played out over the giant Wembley sound system it was incredible.

I was loving this concert and while I was watching it, in my head I was already writing a rave review for The Sun in the knowledge it would appear in Britain's biggest selling national newspaper and would impress the bigwigs at Columbia.

So the following morning, while sat at the showbiz desk at The Sun's Wapping plant in London, with great enthusiasm I set about writing my review of the concert. I raved about it. Describing the atmosphere, the energy and conveying the excitement of being in the audience at the hottest gig in town.

But what I hadn't realised was that Piers was not a fan of Billy Joel. Worse than that, he positively disliked the man. And so when he read my review, Piers decided to make a few changes, adding his personal opinion of the man and not the performance.

It is fair to say that the published review bared little resemblance to the one I had written. In fact, the first three and a half sentences went like this:

"Billy Joel has always struck me as a miserable old devil. He is one of the richest men in pop, he's married to the most beautiful woman in the world and sells millions of records.

"But I've seen more happiness on the face of an orangutan with a spear in its back."

Now you can imagine my shock at reading what was meant to have been a thrilling and joyous review of one of the biggest stars in the world. I knew my contacts at Columbia Records would be fuming when they read this and the chances of getting anymore Press tickets had flown out of the window.

Piers' rewrite continued: "Shuffling on stage at Wembley Arena in his trendy shades, Billy looked a right misery…." And then MY review of the concert kicked in: "…but the show was slick, lively and good value.

"Billy is a hugely talented man and he had the audience rocking from the start. He played all the hits including the classic Uptown Girl. Bizarre rating: An Uptown show Billy!

Ordinarily I would have expected my name to appear under the review. Mercifully, it was left off on this occasion, and so I was able to distance myself somewhat from it.

Still, the headline was positive: "An uptown time with rockin' Billy" and the caption underneath a tiny photograph said: Slick show.

And so the whole review was something of a contradiction and when I first read the published version, I thought Piers Morgan had well and truly ruined my showbiz life.

But it didn't stop me working at The Sun, and I spent a further seven years writing for the Bizarre column. And I do still rather admire Piers Morgan and his incredible career.

I just don't think we'll be sitting down together anytime soon listening to Billy Joel's Greatest Hits.

*Newspaper cutting kindly reproduced with permission from News Licensing.

CHAPTER TWELVE

THE CONNECTICUT CONNECTION

It had been a while since Billy had played in the UK, and I was getting a little impatient. Angry even. Why was I having to wait so long? There was only one thing for it. If Billy wasn't coming to me, then I was going to Billy.

It was 2008 and Billy was embarking on yet another World tour. Except this time, it didn't include Britain. So hardly a World Tour. Tut.

Australia. New Zealand. Japan. Even South Korea. Puerto Rico. Canada. With various dates dotted around the US. But no Wembley. Tut. This was looking expensive.

The US dates didn't include New York City – the quickest, easiest and cheapest option for me coming from the UK. There was one venue that stood out. The Mohegun Sun Arena in a place called Uncasville. I'd never heard of such a place. And certainly couldn't pronounce it. But there must have been something special about this venue. Because on the 2008 tour, he was appearing there no fewer than NINE times. I needed to do some research….

Turns out the Mohegun Sun Casino in Connecticut is owned by the Native American Mohegun Tribe. They filed a Federal land claim suit against the State of Connecticut seeking to reclaim land that had been theirs for an eternity, but was then illegally sold.

As part of the settlement, the Mohegan Nation gained federal recognition by the United States Government in 1994. That year the US Congress passed the *Mohegan Nation (Connecticut) Land Claim Settlement Act.*

Gaining sovereign reservation status enabled the Mohegan Tribe to establish gaming operations on their lands to generate revenue for welfare and economic development. They opened the Mohegan Sun casino on October 12, 1996.

I don't claim to be an expert on Native American tribes, or their investments, but at the time, this appears to have been a shrewd move, bringing wealth and employment to many in the region.

However, during the economic downturn in 2008, much of the expansion was put on hold, with things not picking up again until 2011.

Entertainers who have played the arena include Lucianno Pavarotti, The Who, Tim McGraw, Bob Dylan, Stevie Wonder, The Eagles, Justin Timberlake and Simon & Garfunkel to name but a few.

But one person bringing much needed revenue to the venue was Billy. And what a venue it is. The 10,000 seat Mohegun Sun Arena is a multi-purpose sports and entertainment venue. But why does Billy seem so keen to play here? So I had a look at the map.

It seems the venue is a short private helicopter hop from Billy's Oyster Bay home. Now it's starting to make sense.

And so I book my flight for the end of May 2008, and make my way to New London, Ct.

Once one of the world's busiest whaling ports, New London is home to the United States Coast Guard Academy. The city has a population of about 28,000.

From my room at the Red Roof Inn (or was it the Econo Lodge?), I don't remember there being an awful lot to do in New London. In truth, and with the benefit of hindsight, I probably should have stayed a little closer to the casino. But with concert tickets to purchase, I needed to scrimp on the accommodation.

As is the norm with any Billy Joel gig, it's impossible to get decent tickets without either being blond and beautiful (and thereby gifted a front row seat by Billy's team), a friend of the band, or the Box Office manager. And so I was sat in the nosebleed seats. From what I can recall, it was a great, but rather unremarkable show. However, it was, I believe, one of the first gigs to feature *Highway To Hell*.

But, as it turns out, there WAS something remarkable about this particular Billy Joel trip. Unknown to me at the time, this turned into a Billy Joel Family Fest. And I wanted a seat around the table.

Turns out Billy, his then wife Katie Lee AND daughter Alexa Ray were all in town at the Mohegun Sun for various reasons that weekend; Katie was presenting a Q & A about her new cookbook, The Comfort Table and Alexa was performing a free concert in the bar at the casino called the Wolf Den playing songs from her 2006 CD release, Sketches.

This is Billy Joel heaven. And so it goes. Concert the first night, back the next afternoon to buy another ticket for the concert the following day, before heading into the conference hall for the Katie Lee Q & A.

Now, it's fair to say that I haven't purchased many cookery books in my time, but all of a sudden I'd developed an interest in cookery. There were only about 50 – 60 people who had bothered to attend the Q&A which surprised me. Perhaps people were more interested in gambling than cooking.

Anyway, Katie had the stage set up like a TV studio kitchen, and probably not too dissimilar to her own kitchen set up at home, one would imagine. The conference hall itself probably sat around 500 people, in total, so it was noticeably empty. And so, with the assistance of a helper on stage, she proceeded to prepare some of the recipes from her book. Amazon describes the book perfectly:

"Raised in her grandmother's Southern kitchen, Katie Lee Joel comes from a "family of great cooks and big eaters." And she knows exactly what appeals to the home cook: recipes that are delicious, easy to follow, quick to prepare, and made with readily available seasonal ingredients.

In *The Comfort Table*, Katie dips into her archive of family recipes and updates all the classics from her childhood growing up in West Virginia, and also creates some inventive new favorites. This mouth-watering assortment of more than 125 recipes includes Southern staples like Fried Green Tomatoes, Chicken and Dumplings, Peach Cobbler, Meatloaf, and the quintessential Pulled Pork BBQ, which stand alongside contemporary classics like Roasted Carrot and Ginger Soup, Citrus-Tarragon Mahi-Mahi, and Dijon and Pistachio-Crusted Rack of Lamb.

But *The Comfort Table* is about more than just good old-fashioned home cooking. It›s about sharing delicious, healthful meals -- made with love -- for friends and family. Katie›s rich assortment of recipes for starters, salads, soups, entrees, side dishes, breads, breakfast, desserts, and drinks, is accompanied by entertaining tips and anecdotes to delight the modern foodie. *The Comfort Table* is a comprehensive, unpretentious, refreshingly accessible guide to creating unforgettable meals for occasions big and small."

Now, I don't know if I was simply not that hungry, but most of my attention was on the doors at the rear, around the seats or trying to strain a view backstage. Surely hubby Billy must have been there somewhere to support his wife??

No sign.

The whole cooking thing went completely over my head, and I had little or no interest in learning any recipes.

Anyway, it was time for the Q&A. The chance and opportunity to have a meaningful conversation with a Joel. I was desperately trying to think of a Billy related question to ask Katie. And this was the best I could come up with when the microphone was handed to me:

"Does your husband enjoy eating Elvis Presley sized cheeseburgers?"

I'm not sure where that question came from. Or even what it meant. It didn't raise a laugh. And actually there was an awkward silence. I had nowhere to hide, and mine was the only English accent in the room. The microphone gave out a little whistle. Someone nearby cleared their throat. Awkward.

I can't remember the answer, but it was something along the lines of "I try and cook Billy, healthy, wholesome food, but he does enjoy the odd burger from time to time".

Katie was so gracious in her answer, and throughout her whole presentation, I couldn't help but to think what a lovely person she appeared to be.

Anyway. I didn't see Billy. And I didn't buy her book.

However. Later that evening, it was time to venture into the Wolf Den. A cosy and intimate venue, it had the feel of a small private members club. And so I took my seat early in a booth close to the stage.

This was always going to be an incredible show. If your father is Billy Joel there wasn't going to be anything amateurish about this performance. I wasn't familiar with Alexa's music, but the cool jazz tones, and her sweet pitch perfect voice made for a memorable evening….which was about to get a whole lot more memorable.

Standing just a few feet away from me, with a look of pride on her face that only a mother could have for a daughter was Christie Brinkley. Are you kidding me? Christie. Brinkley. I was in the company of America's favourite supermodel, standing just a few feet away. No entourage. No security. Just a really proud All American Mom.

My attention was now split between watching the show; watching Christie, and keeping an eye out for Billy. This was getting stressful. Was he about to walk on stage and perform a duet with his daughter? And then break into a chorus of *Uptown Girl* for the benefit of Christie? It seemed likely that anything could happen on this trip. My eyes were darting everywhere and head spinning like an excited barn owl as I tried to take it all in.

Surely this was going to be my Billy Joel Moment? I'd invested in flight tickets, concert tickets, and almost a cookery book. This had cost me a fortune. I *deserved* to meet him at this point. It seemed like all the cherries were dropping into place and I must surely hit the jackpot.

I'd seen Billy in concert; interacted (albeit somewhat awkwardly) with his current wife Katie, was a few feet away from daughter Alexa and virtually sat with Christie Brinkley. I was just one piece away from completing the jigsaw.

At the conclusion of Alexa's show, she announced she would be signing copies of her CD in the Casino music store and I obediently went to take my place in the queue.

I graciously told her what a fantastic show it was, and that her father must be very proud that his musical genius had passed to his daughter. Alexa shook my hand and thanked me for my kind words. She asked my name and set about signing a copy of her CD for me. Rather annoyingly, Alexa somehow managed to smudge it using the thick marker pen. I wasn't about to complain and demand another one, or make some stupid Cheeseburger remark again, so I disappeared into the night.

The following evening was concert number two. My seat was worse than the previous show and I was feeling a little deflated that the prize of shaking Billy's hand had so far eluded me.

In one last attempt at a memorable night, midway through the concert, I left my seat up in the Gods and went to the bar to purchase two beers.

Deliberately sloshing the beer over the sides, and with my useless ticket in my mouth and appearing to struggle, I once again attempted to blag my way to the front of the stage.

No luck on this occasion and I made my way back to my useless seat, tail between my legs and spent the remainder of the concert sulking.

I felt I'd come so close on this trip to telling Billy myself just how much his music had influenced my life, but it wasn't to be.

However. I'd met the rest of the Joel clan, even if, at times, I did feel like an unwanted guest at a family wedding.

CHAPTER THIRTEEN

TOMMY BYRNES – GUITAR HERO & HIRED GUN

Guitarist Tommy Byrnes IS rock n roll. He's got all the moves, the gurning facial expressions and a twinkle in his eye.

As Billy Joel's lead guitarist for almost 30 years, he's toured the world several times over and has quite literally been there, got the t-shirt and is living the kind of lifestyle most musicians dream of.

So when I caught up with him at his upstate New York home, I was looking forward to some juicy, tabloid, sex, drugs and rock n roll-style gossip, lifting the lid on life on the road with Billy Joel.

And so for the first time, I can exclusively reveal what legendary axeman Tommy Byrnes likes to do on his days off – er, sweep the yard and pick apples.

That's right folks, the Long Island Music Hall Of Fame Hired Gun winner 2018 likes nothing more than spending some quiet time alone in the garden.

Most definitely the Peter Pan of Rock, 57 year old Tommy easily looks 10 years younger than his age, and is a terrific, nice, down to earth guy. How many more rock n roll clichés can this guy dismiss?

I've met him a couple of times now; the first time was at the launch of the Broadway show *Movin' Out*, then more recently at the June 2018 Manchester concert in the UK where I couldn't see anyone, but we shared a drink in the hotel bar afterwards.

And so when I caught up with him at an intimate Big Shot gig in New York City in October 2018, he said he was happy to be interviewed, but insisted we spend some quality time chatting, rather than catching ten minutes before the show.

And Tommy is a man of his word. We exchanged numbers, and a few days later – after a Billy Joel concert in North Carolina, he's talking to me from his office at home.

What's life like on the road with one of the biggest performers on the planet? I bet you guys are playing jokes, chucking TV's out of windows and generally hellraising:

"We're not as mischievous as we used to be toward one another. We tend to be a bit kinder now that we're all older," says Tommy.

Hmmm. Not quite the answer I was expecting. Surely sound checks must be a chance to let loose and go crazy?

"We show up. Hang out for half an hour before the sound check, then have something to eat and maybe play cards for a while," said Tommy, completely blowing the rock stereotypes right out of the water one after the other.

"It's very relaxed and incredibly casual. Billy will come in a little later, say hello to everyone, we play this and that, check the sound and we're done.

"Billy is very easy to talk to. He'll come into our dressing room and chat about anything. It's never anything serious. It's a happy place."

Tommy recalls: "When I first joined the band I was as nervous as hell. It was a sound check in Los Angeles.

"Afterwards Billy called me into the dressing room with him and he said 'So Tommy, how are you feeling?' I told him my knees were weak at the sound check. He said 'Do you feel better now?' I said yes, and then he poured me a glass of Scotch. He said 'This will take the edge off. Don't worry about it'.

"We used to start the shows with *Angry Young Man* and Billy's line used to be 'Well, we're starting with *Angry Young Man* tonight, so if anybody thinks they're going to make a mistake, they're wrong. I haven't gotten through that intro perfectly in a really long time'."

Nowadays, playing to an audience greater than 50,000 is just another day at the office for Tommy: "There's not too much stress on stage. We're pretty much up there having a good time. If I play a song in the wrong key, it can be pulled out of the mix and probably no-one would notice.

"After all this time you make it as stress free as possible because that's the last thing you want when you're going out there.

"It's a different audience every night and we enjoy the moment because they're enjoying the moment, so we feed off them.

"We've played *Piano Man* a thousand times. The crowd still goes crazy and it's like, okay, we'll do this again. And there are other songs that the radio has beaten to death, that Billy might not want to play, like *Just The Way You Are*.

"I mean it's been covered a thousand times by the biggest artists on the planet, and you go, okay, maybe *Vienna* will take its place tonight. But they all come back. He's got hundreds of songs that he has written and recorded, so there's a deep well to choose from."

Like so many people growing up on Long Island, music has been a part of Tommy's life for as long as he can remember: "I have toured, recorded and written with pretty much everyone who has come off of Long Island at one point of my career; Stray Cat Brian Setzer, Taylor Dayne, Joan Jett.

"But when you get the 'Billy Moment', you kinda go, okay, well there isn't really anybody any bigger, so I'm going to try and hold onto this one.

"When I got the Billy gig, it was definitely a 'holy shit' moment. It floors you. You pinch yourself. You think this is the stuff that happens to other people. I'm incredibly honoured to do this job every night with him."

But while Tommy acknowledges he's living the dream, he never takes it for granted. Not for a moment: "I'm not a rock star. I'm a musician. I know a lot of rock stars. I've worked with a lot of rock stars.

"I think it's very important when you do what I do to always maintain a level head of stability when it comes to living within your means, because nobody knows broke like musicians. We invented it!

"If Billy Joel takes a year off in-between records and touring, Tommy Byrnes still needs to go to work. "I'll go on another tour, or I'll join another band or something, but I got to keep working. Obviously.

"Billy's incredibly generous, but he can stop if he wants, you know, so you gotta remember that. And that's why I don't drive a $200,000 car."

And in complete contrast to former bass player, Larry Russell's experience, Tommy adds: "Working with Billy is a life changer, especially because he is so loyal. He has been incredible to me, and it does, it's like changing your life. It's like winning the musical lottery. He's changed so many different facets of my life too, just by learning his music. He is a master song craftsman."

Over their years together, Billy has learned to trust Tommy's judgement. When the band and set list was revamped in 2006, it was Tommy that Billy consulted.

"He sent me list of maybe 110 songs that he wanted the band to know. I went through them and sent back a list of about 80. We spent probably a month in rehearsal and we played through all of them and then we got down to about 35 and that's what we choose from. I'm quite vocal and outspoken about the songs that drive me crazy.

"There's about 15 songs that you kind of have to play, like *Piano Man* and *Scenes From An Italian Restaurant*. That became most obvious when we were touring with Elton.

"He would go on and do about 13 songs, and we would go on and do the same amount of time, and when you have that to deal with, you have to play the ones you have to play, otherwise the show would be four and a half hours long."

But if Tommy ever doubted Billy's confidence in him, that was confirmed when Billy made him musical consultant for the upcoming Broadway show, *Movin' Out*.

"I always do the best I can for Billy. I'm glad he trusted me to do this and I feel great about it.

"For something like *Movin' Out*, there's nothing better than feeling you can give somebody a job, and to hire 10 musicians was a great feeling. Putting that band together was an amazing thing."

Tommy explained that Michael Cavanaugh, who was to play the lead, was being managed by Billy's tour director at the time, and he insisted that he go and see him in Las Vegas.

And so Tommy arranged for Michael to fly out to New York, and he also recruited Wade Preston for the lead when Michael took days off. "Who was going to play Billy in a show like *Movin' Out* was the hardest position to fill," said Tommy.

"It gave Michael Cavanaugh a completely different career. He went from working in a casino piano bar to working on Broadway, to now playing with symphonies at his own discretion," said Tommy who also cast himself as a band member "....because you never know what is going to happen".

He adds: "You know, I'm a guitar player in a piano band. I'm very fortunate to have the job I have, but to be put in charge of something as monumental as a Broadway show where there are so many millions of dollars being invested, you know you gotta do the right thing all the time."

Billy also put Tommy in charge of producing the Grammy nominated cast album from the show.

"I was thrilled with the arrangements that we came up with for the music, because it did have to change. I didn't quite understand what was going through Twyla's (the choreographer) head because she's that kind of an artist and it's all ballet influence and crazy modern dance.

"There's no narration during the show, nothing explaining what the hell was going on. Basically it was a ballet show set to Billy's music. And so we had the band on stage and I think that was the first time it was ever done. After that you started getting all these what you call Juke Box musicals, and all of a sudden all the bands are on stage."

Following on from the success of *Movin' Out*, does Tommy know if there are any other Broadway shows in the pipeline for Billy?

"There's always talk about resurrecting *Movin' Out*, but it never quite seems to get off the ground.

"I kind of think there's another Broadway moment for Billy, I'm just not sure it will be *Movin' Out*, but I think there could be something else down the line for him. He's open to anything and if anyone has a good idea and it involves his music, he's always willing to listen."

Would Billy ever attempt a Bruce Springsteen style Broadway show, up close and personal with the audience himself?: "I don't know he'll ever venture to that kind of commitment. I haven't seen the Springsteen show, but I think Billy went on the opening night.

"I hear that show is getting longer and longer as Bruce is finding more stuff to talk about. He's like the most dynamic personality.

"He came to our 100th show with us and did *Born To Run*. He just walks out onto that stage and owns it. He definitely knows what to do with anybody's audience."

It was during the *Movin' Out* process, that a certain Michael DelGuidice – who stars and performs in his own Billy Joel tribute act called Big Shot, was brought to Tommy's attention: "Billy was calling me about DelGuidice because he really wanted him to do *Movin' Out*.

"He had seen Michael's website and he was like 'This guy sounds exactly like me. He's gotta be in the show'.

"And so I called Michael and went to see him live a couple of times in clubs on Long Island and he was amazing, but every time he showed up to audition for us it was 11am, and he had just done five shows in a row and he was hoarse.

"And I'm sitting there with Twyla and we're like 'arghh'. We'd all seen him on the web, but we thought he's not going to survive this because it was really disciplined and you couldn't do anything else.

"I've told Michael, it would have been cool if he did *Movin' Out* because we're really good friends now, and we obviously tour together with Billy, and play together with Big Shot, and I told him 'Look at it this way. You're in the band. And if you had taken *Movin' Out*, it would have been a pay cut, trust me'. Michael does really well. Big Shot's a big friggin band.

"I'm talking about DelGuidice by the way. Cavanaugh was like Captain Broadway. He lapped it up and he was great at it too. I remember seeing him do his first TV interview, and I was like 'Dude. It's like you've been doing that all your life'. He was perfect for it."

And it's in between the big gigs that Tommy finds himself supporting DelGuidice in his band Big Shot: "It feels great. I already know the songs and don't have to rehearse!

"I get treated pretty nicely too, cos Billy's not there! The pat on the back from fans once in a while is fun. We enjoy the music and we can play what we want. It's a Billy tribute band, but we do a lot of other stuff.

"It's a little harder when we do a rarities show. Billy's music isn't that easy, and we screw up 90 per cent of that stuff. You could never get Billy to play half of those songs because he thinks 'Nahh. People will go to the bathroom'".

But Billy's popularity shows no signs of slowing down, with his run of sold out shows at Madison Square Garden continuing. What does Tommy put this continued surge in Billy's popularity down to?

"Billy's in The Circle. There's a Circle and it's very small and there are not that many people that are in it. You get to a point in your career, which Billy has reached. He's Sinatra-esque.

"The Rolling Stones are in that Circle. U2 are in that Circle. Paul McCartney is in that Circle. Anyone who can sell out Wembley and The Garden are in that Circle. You've gotta do it on both sides of The Pond though."

Turning to the former Beatle, Tommy adds: "Paul has a few years on Billy. He's been singing high all his life and he hasn't lowered the keys as he's gotten older. He still sings *Maybe I'm Amazed* in the key he wrote it in. That's crazy.

"I think he does damage. Billy might do three shows a month, but never more than one a week because of that specific thing.

"I think Billy could do it forever, as far as the audience goes, but as far as he's concerned, he'll only do it for as long as he feels he is doing a good job.

"I know he said he would continue the run at The Garden every month until it wasn't sold out. And so five years later, it's showing no signs of slowing down. It's selling out faster than ever. I think it's one of those moments of 'Did I really say that? Somebody kick me'".

"If he felt he was not capable, for one reason or another, playing or singing, he would walk away from it, because I think he would rather not play if it wasn't as good as it could be. Some of his songs are pretty physical".

I steal a moment during the interview to tell Tommy about our experience of the doomed Manchester gig in the UK.

"Oh. You were one of those people who couldn't see the heads. Couldn't see anything? We heard all about that.

"It was all the talk at the next show. It was like 'Holy shit. What the hell happened?' I don't know exactly what happened, but Billy would never want to do that.

"Any restricted seats don't get sold. I'm sorry you had the shitty seats though. Yeah, we all heard about it, trust me."

Tommy's contribution to the Long Island music scene was officially recognised this year when he was inducted into the Long Island Music Hall of Fame.

"The first thing I did was go online and see who else was in there. I was blown away by the amount of people and the diversity of music that has come off of Long Island. People who have completely changed the face of music all from one spot," said Tommy.

And the honour was given the official seal of approval when Long Island's most famous son, Billy Joel himself, inducted Tommy at a star studded ceremony.

But Tommy isn't the first Billy Joel band member to receive the honour, Liberty DeVitto, Richie Cannata and Russell Javors are also inductees.

Drummer Liberty even featured in a controversial movie called The Hired Gun. Tommy says of his former band mate: "I saw the movie.

"I'm not sure what Liberty thinks of me, but he was one of my favourite people. I lived with him for 15 years. We toured every day. We used to do the big long world tours when you'd be gone for six weeks, home for seven days over the course of a year and a half. Around the world. Over and over again.

"He was one of the funniest guys I knew. A good mentor. Those are things I could not take away from him. I don't know what the exact cause of the rift between him and Billy was. But that wasn't mine to have or to understand at that time."

And so away from the glare of the spotlights, what's life like for Tommy Byrnes?: "I live about 90 miles north of Manhattan. I had a place in New York City for a few years, but we moved up here off Long Island when my kids were young.

"I go back there all the time and was there recently with my daughter. She said 'How can you deal with this? We've gone five miles in the last hour and a half'. I said this is Long Island and this is why we don't live here anymore!"

Explain again about that lifestyle between shows: "I'm outside all the time. I love working in the yard. I've got so much cleaning up to do now the Fall is here. So I can be out there for two days.

"I cut down an apple tree the other day with my chainsaw and made apple sauce with my shoes. It's insane! I never saw a bigger mess in my life! I love working outside. There's always something to clean up in the yard, and my wife's garden is ridiculous. The two of us spend a lot of time out there."

Tommy has two children, 28 year old TJ and 26 year old Bonnie.

"They have lived away and gone to school, and moved back home, and gotten apartments, then moved back home. I call them my baby boomerangs!

"My daughter sings. We recorded a record for her with my son who is a recording engineer and a writer, singer and player. So we have done a lot of stuff and recorded a lot of music together," says Tommy.

But is it a career he would recommend?: "Only if it works! If it works, great. It's a really, really competitive area and they know that which is why the both have jobs."

Finding out about Tommy's life has been fascinating. But not particularly easy. You see, there is very little on the internet about Tommy Byrnes.

Visiting the Billy Joel website takes you to a page about the individual band members. Click on their names and you're re-directed to their own personal websites. Click on Tommy's name and you get a photo and the words: Guitars. Vocals.

"I have no interest in Google. Whatever you saw up there, I had nothing to do with that," says a typically modest Tommy.

And so finally, Long Island Music Hall of Famer Tommy Byrnes' story is officially out there, and I feel honoured that I'm the one telling it. Rock n Roll, baby. Yeah!

CHAPTER FOURTEEN

MOVIN' OUT (MICHAEL'S SONG) - THE GIG THAT CHANGED HIS LIFE

There are very few people who can boast of sharing a hotel suite with Billy Joel. But Michael Cavanaugh is one of them.

Michael is the uber talented musician who went from Piano Bars to Broadway overnight after Billy Joel handpicked him to star in the hit show, *Movin' Out*. It's the kind of rock n roll story that people dream of, but this was reality for Michael.

For those of you not familiar with the show, Wikipedia sums it up nicely:

Movin' Out is a 2002 musical featuring the songs of Billy Joel. Conceived by choreographer Twyla Tharp, the musical tells the story of a generation of American youth growing up on Long Island during the 1960s and their experiences with the Vietnam War.

The principal characters are drawn from those who appeared in various Joel tunes: high school sweethearts Brenda and Eddie (*Scenes from an Italian Restaurant*), James (*James*), Judy (*Why Judy Why*), and Tony (Anthony in *Movin' Out*).

The show is unusual in that, unlike the traditional musical, it essentially is a series of dances linked by a thin plot, and none of the dancers sing. All the vocals are performed by a pianist (Michael Cavanaugh) and band suspended on a platform above the stage while the dancers act out the songs' lyrics, making the show, in essence, a rock ballet.

I was lucky enough to catch up with Michael via Skype at his Las Vegas home where he told me the incredible story of how he overcame career threatening surgery and crippling nerves to land "the gig that changed his life":

Las Vegas 2001. Michael Cavanaugh is making a name for himself at the piano playing three shows a day in the Duelling Piano Bar at the New York New York Hotel and Casino. Its standing room only show after show as even the most hardened gamblers turn their backs on the slots to check out the hottest musician on the world famous Strip. And word is spreading.

Michael takes up the story: "I'd got to know Billy's tour manager, Max Loubiere. Max and I were friends before I met Billy and Max and I decided that we wanted to work together.

"I knew Billy was coming into town for a concert with Elton, but I wasn't expecting a call from Max 15 minutes before I left home for work. Max said "I'm bringing Billy to your show".

"At first I didn't believe him. I thought: "Billy Joel's not going to a piano bar. He's too famous." So I was driving to the casino like a maniac, freaking out thinking Billy Joel *might* be coming to see me. I get another call from Max saying they're gonna be there in five minutes.

"I go to the back of the casino and they pull up in the car and there he is. Billy said to me: "Are you Mike? Nice to meet you. Relax." And I did. I immediately relaxed. So we're walking toward the piano bar and he says: "So what kind of music do you play here?" And I said "Well we certainly play a lot of yours".

Word was getting out that Billy was in town. And as the anticipation was building that Billy might join in on the duelling pianos, Michael was trying to keep it together.

"We tried to keep it a secret he was coming into the bar but we were unsuccessful. We had to clear out a booth and people wanted to know why.

"So I walked in with Billy and everyone starts screaming because they see Billy Joel walk in. I must have relaxed because I leaned over toward him and said: "Let's get one thing straight, they're not screaming for you, they're screaming for me" and he laughed. He patted me on the back and I sat at the piano and got all nervous again because he was like eight feet away from me. And I remember thinking "I'm not gonna play any Billy Joel in front of Billy Joel. There's no way", but of course, that's all anybody wanted to hear."

Teasing the crowd, Michael opened his set that night with Elton's *Saturday Night's Alright For Fighting*.

"Everyone was wanting Billy Joel," said Michael, and I thought "Nope. Not playing it. No way." So Michael played one of his own original tunes, and as he did, looked at the Piano Man for reassurance: "That was nerve wracking to say the least, but Billy told me he liked it, so that was good.

"Then everyone is yelling for *Piano Man* and I think "I can't play *Piano Man* in front of Billy Joel". The whole place is screaming "*PIANO MAN*" and of course they really want Billy to sing it, but they're thinking that's never gonna happen. I look over at him and he waves like "Ahh go ahead". So I get out the harmonica and I don't use the holder. So my wife is there and he says to her "How can he do it without the thing?" The funny thing is, I can't do it with the thing. I feel like Frankenstein wearing that thing.

"So, I'm playing *Piano Man* and Billy was singing along like everyone else. After that Max comes over and whispers to me "Hey do you want Billy to sit in?" because it's like duelling pianos and I'm like "YES. Are you kidding me?"

"Billy comes up on stage and says to me "Do you know *With A Little Help From My Friends*. I'm like "Absolutely. Yes" He sings the first verse, then he points to me for the second verse and so I sing the second verse and then we're singing harmonies with each other. I can't believe this is really happening. After that we did the Elvis tune *Don't Be Cruel* and it was amazing."

Michael had no idea that this encounter would lead to anything. He says: "I didn't know *Movin' Out* was even a thing yet, but it was already in the works and the plan was there. Tommy Byrnes (Billy's long time guitarist) who I also met that week, Billy had said to Tommy, I want you to put the band together for this thing because I know if you do it, it'll be done the right way. So Tommy said to Billy "I think Cavanaugh is the perfect guy for this" Billy said: "He's great. Sounds good to me". So I had Billy's thumbs up!

Billy liked Michael, but the brains of the show was creator Twyla Tharp, and he still had to win her over to secure the gig. "And if she had not liked me, trust me, it would never have happened," says Michael.

Later that year the show starts to come together, and Michael finds himself in New York City: "We first started working on the show it was right after 9/11.

"I flew to New York for the workshop, I think it was September 23 2001 and I thought they were going to cancel everything because 9/11 had just happened. I didn't know if it was going to move forward or not. I was amazed by the strength of New Yorkers.

"I rehearsed with Twyla and the dancers for a week before the band even came and there was a lot happening. And then we did our three workshop performances for the investors and for Billy Joel and his people.

"I was so nervous it was crazy. (Billy's tour manager) Max told Billy "Michael's flipping out" so Billy came up to me and gave me a big hug and said: "Hey don't worry about it and don't worry about mistakes". I'm glad he said that because we were doing Uptown Girl and I completely started singing the wrong lyrics. I looked over at him and he looked at me and was like (laughs). I then totally relaxed and it was great.

With the workshops a great success, Michael could relax. He recalls: "I remember I hung out with Billy after the workshop. He was staying at the St

Regis and he had an amazing suite on the top floor and he said: "Where are you staying?" and I said: "the Doubletree" and he was like, "Ahh. Ok. I've decided I want to go home tonight to Long Island. Do you want my suite?" and I said "Sure" and he gave me his suite!.

And that, Billy Joel fans, is how Michael Cavanaugh became the only musician in history to share a hotel suite with the Piano Man himself.

With financial backing now approved and in place, slowly the production started to come together, and in June of 2002, the show opened in Chicago for pre-Broadway audiences.

Michael remembers: "I was so green when it came to Broadway. I had no idea how hard it was to have a hit Broadway show. I thought this is Billy Joel in New York, he can't lose.

"In Chicago people at first had trouble with the storyline and then I realised how quickly shows closed and then I got real nervous. My contract was a year-long. And then I remember the producers told me "well if we don't get good reviews in Chicago, we'll be closed by Thanksgiving. Fortunately the reviews were fantastic and the whole thing worked out great. I was focused on doing the best job I could. I knew it was a different kind of Broadway musical, for sure.

"I remember when we got to New York we were still making changes and I was having lunch with Billy in New York and we talked about his song *Half A Mile Away* and he starts singing it at the table with me and I thought I can't believe this is happening. I'm having lunch with Billy and he's singing one of the songs to me at the table from my all-time favourite album which is *52nd Street* and I'm thinking "this is pretty amazing".

"He's very friendly, but you gotta understand, everywhere he goes, every second of everyday people are dropping their forks to just gawk at him when he's trying to eat his food. He really is a good guy. But that spotlight just never goes out. He handles it probably better than I would."

Things were going well. Michael's one year contract became two, then three and Michael relocated his family from Florida to Glen Rock, New Jersey.

But the punishing schedule was taking its toll on Michaels' voice. And what many people didn't know was that when he was 18, Michael had a delicate operation on his vocal chords to remove growths…and there were fears at the time he would never sing again.

"When I started in the first year, I did six shows, six days a week, and the second cast which featured Wade Preston, would do the matinees on Saturday and Wednesdays, and on the shows I played the lead he would do synthesiser.

"It was a tough gig vocally. It was very tough because I sang the whole thing and doing it six days a week I remember even Billy was like: "Man you got a tough gig! Do you know what you've signed up for?"

But the more I screamed, the more Twyla (choreographer) loved it."

Once the show established itself in New York, Michael says Billy was pretty much "hands on".

"Once we got to New York, Billy came around quite a bit. I remember I was singing the wrong lyric on *She's Got A Way* for the first six months of the show and Billy finally decided he was going to tell me. It was small. I think I'd sang "Don't know what it is" instead of "don't know why it is". I can't quite remember but it was small. He didn't want to tell me and he felt bad, but I thought no please tell me.

"But yeah. He was hands on and he would come to a lot of the shows and do the encore, *New York State of Mind* and it was amazing. He did that maybe a dozen times. And when he did it, they wrote about it in the papers. It was a big deal."

I travelled to New York and saw the show a few months into the opening run. And I can remember blagging some pretty hot tickets to an after show party. I remind Michael of this: "Ahh the Supper club gig.

"I didn't get paid for that gig! The venue had a couple of different names and me and a bunch of guys from the *Movin' Out* band were booked to play there and they wanted it to be once a month. We thought that would be really cool and we did it. My manager was saying we shouldn't do this gig. I was like "it'll be fine" and I'd already paid all the guys in the band.

"I did get paid two weeks late and then the place closed. Tommy (Byrnes) played in *Movin' Out* and he was there. He put the whole band together and had the freedom to do whatever he wanted to do. Tommy's a fun guy."

About 18 months into the season, Michael got sick. He explains: "About a year and a half in it started to take its toll on me. I got bronchitis and Wade from the second cast got sick the same time I did."

Michael thinks cross contamination on the shared keyboard was to blame. He explains: "The crew were supposed to disinfect the piano, but I'm not sure they always did. So one of us would do a show and then (coughs) and so the other guy was getting it!"

Determined "the show must go on", Michael started to feel the strain on his vocal chords: "For a few weeks I was cheating my vocal techniques because I was sick.

"When you're sick or when an athlete is hurt, they start cheating the way they do things to get over it, so it kind of messed me up." Michael describes this as his "bump in the road".

"To help me, I started studying with a vocal coach called Joan Lader who to this day is still my vocal coach over FaceTime. She's worked with the biggest stars on Broadway and the biggest stars in the world. Everyone from Madonna to Paul Simon. Joan Lader pulled me out of the trenches when I hit that tough spot. She keeps me in good shape."

The show ran for more than three years on Broadway to rave reviews. That's a lot of shows. Michael says: "I kept a running total for a while, but I lost count. It was roundabout a thousand shows, maybe a few short. It was three years and a couple of months in NY and if you count the pre-Broadway in Chicago it was three and a half years. It was a long time.

Nominated for a Grammy AND a Tony. How did that make Michael feel?: "It made me feel great!

"Unfortunately we lost them both. There was so much going on during the Tony's in terms of media and interviews. When they read my name as a nominee, I hadn't written a speech and I was really starting to freak out. When they read out the winner, at first I felt relief, but 30 seconds later, it was like "oh man". It was incredible. I knew when I got nominated for the Tony and Grammy it was something I was going to have for the rest of my life. It was amazing. Incredible.

"I remember on the very last show we did, the last song before the encore was called *I've Loved These Days* and I remember I changed the last verse without talking to anybody, including Billy. I can remember what I did. Something like "One more time upon the stage until we turn the final page" and everyone was crying and then Billy comes up on stage for the encore and he whispers in my ear "Hey. I noticed the new lyrics". I said "Oh man. I hope that didn't bother you? He said "Nah. It's alright".

And then it felt that as quickly as it started, it all came to an end. The show moved briefly to London, but it didn't enjoy the same success seen on Broadway.

I wondered how things had been left with Billy?: "Billy has been great," said Michael. "I haven't seen him since last year. The last time he was in Vegas I took my whole family to the show. I wasn't expecting him to do any more than say hello but for 20 minutes right before he went on stage he hung out with me and my family backstage. He has always been supportive."

But what was life like for Michael before *Movin' Out*?

The youngest of four boys, Michael is from a musical family from Cleveland, Ohio, and while he says his parents never pushed them into performing in an Osmonds-style band, he did team up with his brother Tom in the early days.

"I'm the only one crazy enough to make a living at this", says Michael. "I played in a band with my brother Tom when I was a teenager for a while in the late 80s. Top 40 stuff. I played synthesizer."

How much did Billy Joel influence the young Michael Cavanaugh?

"I love how eclectic he is. He covers it all both lyrically and musically. A song like *Big Shot*. As a kid I didn't realise he was singing it to himself. But it was like this pissed off rock tune and then you hear *Don't Ask Me Why*, something so completely different.

"I was thinking 'Is this the same guy?' Wow. I've loved the variety in his styles. He's an incredible story teller. When you look at song writer, performer, singer, whole package. He's pretty tough to beat. Him and guys like Paul McCartney – he's in that same league. He was my favourite artist from a very young age. Especially as a teenager. When I played in that Top 40 band I would play *Honesty* and *She's Got A Way* in these dance clubs, and it would be the slow dance. I was about 14 at the time and playing in clubs four nights a week. I've been at it a long time."

It was when Michael turned 18 he had the surgery on his voice to remove nodules: "I didn't perform for a year but it all turned out fine," he says. Unsure if he would be able to make a career out of music, Michael trained as a piano tuner before resuming the singing career.

Married at 21, Michael and his young family moved to Orlando when he was 22. Four and a half years later his son was born and shortly after that came the Vegas job offer and his family relocated there in 1998.

And Vegas is still the place he calls home: "It's not so bad. I tell people my family and I sleep under the slot machines that aren't so loud.

"I can see the strip from my bedroom window, but it's another world. Where I live it's much more like living in Scotsdale. My neighbour across from me is a lawyer, the guy over there is a Cop. The guy next to me is a pilot. Everyone is in bed before the 11 O'clock news. It's as normal as normal can be.

"When I go to the strip, I feel like a tourist every time I go. I either go to The Strip once in a while to see a show, or I'll do a gig there. Other than that, I don't go. I live in Henderson and Henderson is very safe. There's no smutty billboards or anything like that. It's a family atmosphere here and it's great. It doesn't really matter where I live, because I just keep getting on airplanes for a living. And I'm not a gambler. That's *why* I can live here."

Looking back at more than a thousand performances of *Movin' Out*, how much of a Billy Joel fan is Michael now, or does he think "If I hear *Piano Man* one more time I'm gonna BLOW...."?

"No. That did not happen. I am still just as big as a Billy Joel fan as ever. But if I have to hear the *Movin' Out* soundtrack one more time, then I could lose my mind.

"I would tell people the best way to get me to leave a party was to put on the *Movin' Out* soundtrack. But to me hearing Billy sing *Scenes From An Italian Restaurant* or *Movin' Out*, or *The Stranger*, I still love it. And every time I hear it, I think: "He's still the best." I think he's still writing. But he just wants to write for himself now."

And so Michael Cavanaugh nowadays is about his hugely successful Symphony Orchestra shows: "The first time I played with a symphony was in Carnegie Hall. Talk about a way to get broken in. I remember I opened the show with *New York State Of Mind* and then I did an Elton John song called *Bad Blood* he did with Neil Sedaka and Neil was there.

"We were approached by the Indianapolis symphony. They had seen me on Broadway. They wanted to do a show. I did shows for them and it has been amazing. We've been all over the US and Canada. I would love to do it in the UK, that's for sure.

"Billy has been great. He knows I'm doing these shows with symphonies performing his stuff and doing Elton's stuff."

Looking easily ten years younger than his 46 years, he puts his youthful looks down to yoga, healthy eating "because we are what we eat", and... Just For Men "I'd look like Kenny Rogers if I grew a beard".

And so my time with Michael was coming to an end. And, as we say in jolly old England, he's a thoroughly decent chap.

And you can see for yourself - Michael documents his antics with a series of video diaries available on You Tube.

CHAPTER FIFTEEN

LARRY RUSSELL PART THREE - SIGMA – THE REUNION

Fast forward to 2011, and Larry gets wind of news that the Sigma Studios session has been dusted off and is to be made available for the first time as part of a re-release of the 1973 album *Piano Man*. Branded the "Legacy Edition" it features a bonus CD of the Sigma Studios session in its entirety.

Larry picks up the story: "So, I get a call from Columbia Records and they want to interview me to promote the album," says Larry. "You think they would pay me then, but nothing gets paid.

"But I was so excited, because I thought finally. Finally we're gonna be known; something is gonna come out. How long does it take? 50 years before this gets uncovered?

"So we're talking to lawyers and they made an offer. The offer was four times the price of what the union would pay a side man. A side man. Isn't that sad? So the whole premise of Billy saying 'This is a band' is bullshit. So, we only got, after tax was taken out, $1,300 each.

"Share some of the wealth, Billy. Do you need every penny? Give us some grown up money. $1,300? This isn't grown up money. He could have said 'You know what. I have this bill I should pay'. It was an emotional debt he didn't pay and that bothers me.

"Al Hertzberg said to me years ago that it's one thing not getting recognition. It's another thing not being paid, but having both happen to you, it's the worst."

"But I accepted it for one reason. I thought this is my chance. This is our chance for us to be known. Let's see what we can make of it.

Larry came up with the concept of a live Sigma reunion show. But once again, it was Billy and Larry's mutual friend Jeff Schock who was in the driving seat.

Jeff, who passed away in November 2017, was very firmly part of the Billy Joel inner sanctum and one of Billy's closest lieutenants. He was also the creator and guardian of the Billy Joel Archive. Anything Jeff did, had Billy's blessing.

Larry explains: "Jeff made this happen. He met me. And we talked and he felt my pain. He went to CBS and told them 'We gotta do this. This is great'. Columbia own everything and they had the master tape of the Sigma recording.

"But Jeff went to Billy, because Billy had to sign off on everything, and Billy said to Jeff 'What's this all about?' And Jeff told him. And Billy said 'Whatever'.

"I'm sorry. Billy had his chance at that moment. Instead of saying "whatever", he could have said 'You know what, let's give each one of those guys points (a percentage). If this was Bruce Springsteen, he would have done that. Billy didn't do the right thing. He still doesn't know how to do the right thing."

And so in early 2011, Larry started to put the Sigma reunion together, in support of the release of the recording, in the hope that he and the band would finally get some recognition….and that ultimately Billy would give his seal of approval and acknowledge the contribution they made to his career.

However, the economy was still recovering from the financial crash, and it wasn't until 2013 that Larry was able to put things in motion.

Firstly Larry reconnected with drummer Rhys Clark. Unfortunately Al Hertzberg couldn't make it due to health reasons, but he was replaced by Don Evans who was the original guitarist on the *Cold Spring Harbor* album.

"I never approached Billy to be a part of the reunion," said Larry. "I approached him to come. He wouldn't perform and I wouldn't even think of having him do that. But just to be in the audience. To support us. Could he at least do that?"

And so the search was on to find a replacement "Billy".

"I needed to find someone who could sing like Billy and could play like him. It's very hard. The beats Billy played with us were like classical music and it's hard to find someone who can play those beats and sing at the same time. Billy was unbelievable then. Remember *Rosalinda*? How great was that? Incredible. I mean how do you sing and play like that?"

Even now, probably without realising it and despite all the upset, angst and scars those early years have left, Larry can't help but admire his former band mate, and pay tribute to his talent.

So Larry started investigating and researching Billy Joel tribute bands worldwide, and it occurred to him that he could have more than one "Billy".

And finally his search was narrowed to just three contenders who all stood out above the others. They were Mike Delguidice, David Clark and Britain's Elio Pace.

"I found Mike first because I thought his voice sounded just like Billy's. I sent him the tapes but wasn't getting any feedback, and I realised that he didn't want to do it.

"So I found David and I thought 'Wow. He's good'. Has good dexterity – not like Billy, but he's not bad. Great voice, a little like a "later" Billy."

Larry was introduced to Elio Pace via Tony Walker, a prominent member of the Billy Joel Completely Retold Facebook group.

"I called Elio and we ended up talking on the phone for four hours. I could tell he really wanted to do it.

"When Elio performs there's real love. When Billy does it, he's thinking 'Kerching. I'll get $2million tonight'. He only does it for money. That's my theory."

Originally Larry tried to raise $80,000 to cover the costs of these unique shows, to fly people around and make sure people got a paycheck. "I wanted to pay everyone properly, not the way Billy handled it."

But the cash simply wasn't there. Larry managed to find a small amount of sponsorship to pay for rehearsals, artwork and printing.

Larry recalls that emotional first rehearsal: "I went upstairs and the door flew open, and there's Rhys. There's a picture of us hugging. And when we started playing the first chords of *Captain Jack*, it was like playing with Billy again. Rhys and I sound great together. Forty five years can go by, and yet it's still there. It was fantastic."

A total of just five reunion shows were played – two in 2013 and three in 2014 in New York City, Philadelphia and Delaware. Billy himself didn't make any of the shows, but Jeff Schock did.

"Billy didn't come to the show for one reason: he didn't know what it was going to sound like. I just think that he didn't want to be in a position that, if it sucked, he couldn't tell us. In that way, he's not a phoney.

"But he could have said to us: 'Go guys. I'm here to support you. Great memories. I remember that'. But he didn't do that. He could have sent a recorded message, but he doesn't have that kind of compassion. He doesn't care because he doesn't have to. Just be in the audience. Support us. Could he at least not do that?

"Jeff loved it. He said 'Oh my God, this sounds great'. I'm not sure if Billy sent him, or Jeff wanted to be there to document this because he was the archivist. But he was there and he loved it."

Larry admits it was a blow that Billy didn't make any of the shows, but he adds: "Putting on those shows had nothing to do with his appearance. In fact, I had to write down that he was not going to be there. Jeff made me do that.

"You know what the weird thing is? The week or the weeks before the show, I said to Jeff 'Put something on the Billy Joel (web) site. Billy puts his daughter's gigs on there.

"It's actually unbelievable. It's a pattern of neglect. A pattern of ungratefulness. He doesn't think it's important. He doesn't think we're important. He thinks he's important."

Those lucky enough to have got tickets for the reunion shows were not disappointed, and the reviews, sold out signs and standing ovations reflected this. Larry has produced an 18 minute taster clip which is available on You Tube. Elio Pace still says being asked to take part in the shows was one of the best moments of his life.

And while Larry is rightly proud of the success of the shows and the memories it evoked, that love/hate bitterness won't leave him alone.

We turn our attention to the Lords of 52nd Street – the tribute band which features former Billy Joel band members Liberty DeVitto, Richie Cannata and Russell Javors, with David Clark filling in on keyboard and vocals.

Larry had issues with the Lords when they initially referred to themselves as the "original" Billy Joel band.

"So I wrote to Liberty. This was about a year ago," says Larry, "and first of all I said 'you're not the original band', and he said 'well, we're the ones that had the most hits'.

"I said 'Original means order of appearance. We were there first'. So they stopped with their advertising.

"Do they need to be the "original" band? They made the money. They had the hits. Now they're the Legends Of The Billy Joel Band. And that's fine. But don't call yourself 'Original'.

But then out of the blue, says Larry, he gets a call from a mutual friend asking if he wants to be a part of the Lords. "They caught me by surprise," said Larry. "And I thought, I don't know. I thought maybe. But then I thought 'I don't want to'.

"I don't want to be unhappy. I don't fit in with those guys. I just don't. It's not my tenure. My tenure was the beginning. I don't want to muck it up and I don't want to combine. It makes no sense. Then they'll say it was the original because I'm in the band.

"It would have been good money, and believe me, I can always use money. But I thought about how I'd feel.

"Every time I see or hear a live version of *Captain Jack*, I go 'Ughhh', it's awful. It's kind of like someone else going out with your girlfriend. That's how music is. It gets into your heart and is so much a part of you."

And so, after four hours of fascinating conversation and food, our time together is coming to an end. But I can't resist one last question:

I ask: "So Larry. Tell me. What would you do if Billy Joel walked in here right now?"

"Knowing me, I'd have to say something, but fear I might be rejected, too," is Larry's honest response.

"He might say 'Oh', but he might make the best of it to save face. I've not seen him in a while. The last time I saw him was in a club called Tracks. It was May 4, 1980. I had heard he was coming in and I had just got back from a tour. I got up on stage and we played together.

"But Billy's angry with me because he thought I was trying to sue him. It would be nice for Billy to say something like 'Larry. Don't worry. I've had time to think about this, and we're not going to be here forever'."

One week later, and Sharon and I return to the City Diner for dinner and a catch up with Larry. He has his neighbour with him called Ted.

This time the conversation is off the record, and we are fascinated to hear about Larry's life before Billy; about his time spent hanging out at Judy Garland's place with her daughters Liza Minnelli and Lorna Luft and the friendship they had.

If talking to Larry can be described as fun, then listening to him speak is fascinating. He has an incredible memory for dates, and loves to tell a story. He would be a great guest on a TV chat show; he says what he thinks and doesn't hold back.

But it doesn't take long for the conversation to get back to Billy. The love and admiration he feels for his former band mate is overwhelming. And the sadness he feels that the relationship has broken down is plain to see.

While it's clear that Larry feels Billy owes him a few bucks for services rendered during the early seventies, it is also blatantly clear that if he had just an ounce of the recognition he feels he was owed and robbed of for the undoubted contribution he made in the early days, he could put the Billy Joel chapter of his life to bed.

Who knows, after reading this book, maybe Billy will make it out for that Italian meal with Larry that Jeff had been promising, share a memory and acknowledge the old days. If that happens, I'd expect an invitation. And the least Billy could do would be to pick up the cheque. I'll meet you anytime you want, in an Italian restaurant.

CHAPTER SIXTEEN
IT'S STILL ROCK N ROLL TO HIM

ELIO PACE performing The Billy Joel Songbook is no two-bit tribute act. It's not some lookey-likey singing karaoke style to an *Uptown Girl* backing track.

There are no cliché's with Elio Pace. Just class.

When I saw the advertisement for The Billy Joel Songbook at The Stables music venue in Milton Keynes, the inner Billy Joel in me laughed. I was actually insulted. I never believed Billy was worthy of an end-of-pier style show. He was much better than that. I believed that if people hadn't discovered the brilliant music of the Angry Young Piano Man by now, they should be denied the privilege.

I wasn't going to go to this concert. I couldn't stand to see the work of my hero reduced to karaoke cabaret with some bloke wearing Ray Ban specs trying to sing *Tell Her About It* badly. And I should know, I've tried – and failed – to sing that song myself at karaoke and it ain't easy.

But hang on a minute. £19 a ticket. Mmmm. It's worth paying that just to heckle. It's worth paying that to laugh. It's worth paying that to mock the disbelievers. And worth paying that to wear my 1984 Tour shirt because no-one else would have one. Pah.

I was so convinced this was going to be the biggest, insulting pile of crap you could imagine, I didn't even bother taking Mrs B. I wasn't prepared to subject her to such benign nonsense. I decided to take my mate Max. He's ex-army and likes a pint or two. Just the sort of companion I needed to throw some drunken heckles out there on my behalf.

The Stables is an intimate venue, attracting a discerning crowd, seating about 500. Originally opened by Cleo Laine and the late Johnny Dankworth. The venue was sold out.

Any artist appearing at this venue needs to work hard to get a reaction. They expect the highest standards and take no prisoners if the act is second rate. This show was SO gonna bomb and I couldn't wait.

As I took my seat, in silent protest, the first thing that struck me was the equipment laid out on stage – a Baby Grand piano. Impressive drum kit. Good array of guitars, keyboards and saxophone. Not a playback machine in sight. I was convinced this was going to be a case of "all the gear, but no idea".

Despite the sell-out, the crowd sat in silence. The house lights dimmed. Not a sound. Elio and his full band walked out onto the stage. Silence. Elio pulled the stool out from beneath the piano, scrapping the legs on the wooden floor. There was some slight feedback from a mike. Still silence.

The spotlight fell on Elio, and he postured himself over the keyboard. Oh how I yawned.

But then it started. His hands a blur. This man, Elio Pace, had the damned temerity, the bare faced cheek to pick the standard Billy Joel concert opener to start his own show. The ultra-complicated, high speed opening to *Angry Young Man* was being played in front of my eyes. Was he pretending? Was he really playing? And then the rest of the band joined in.

OH MY GOD. This was incredible. Was I actually watching the real thing at the MGM Grand in Las Vegas? It bloody well sounded like it.

Talk about an opening. And this set the standard for the rest of the show – 40 Billy Joel songs; hits, deep album cuts, standard classics. For example; *New York State of Mind.* Sang at the piano, played note perfect, sang pitch perfect. Reproduced to the very highest musical standard. Billy himself would have been proud.

In fact, dare I say it, Billy himself would struggle to reach some of those notes which were effortlessly performed by Elio.

In-between songs, Elio talked passionately about his love of Billy Joel. He described how he first discovered the *Innocent Man* album after being dumped by his girlfriend at the time, and the track *This Night*, which changed his life.

In fact, he says after hearing this song, his life took a swerve.

Elio knew his stuff. But what was even more frustrating was he put his skills quite literally where his mouth was, and with his band re-produced note perfect hit after hit after hit.

From the frosty reception he got when first walking on stage, by the time *Uptown Girl* came on EVERYONE was on their feet dancing.

Talk about a turnaround. I was not expecting this.

After the show Max and I hung out in the bar. I was secretly waiting to meet the man who had brought Billy's music to life right here in my home town of Milton Keynes, while Max sunk another couple of pints.

Sure enough, 10 minutes later and Elio appeared, happily signing CDs and chatting to fans not just about himself, but about Billy too. We chatted. I bought a CD and Elio signed it. What a thoroughly decent chap….and just the kind of person I needed to talk to for this project. Quite clearly Billy had touched Elio's life in some way and I felt sure he would be happy to talk about it. But now wasn't the time to ask him.

When I got home I was buzzing. Sharon could see the excitement on my face as I told her about the show. Out came the laptop. Where was Elio playing next? Dunstable. Booked. Potters Bar. Booked. Eastbourne. Booked. Weston Super Mare. Booked.

Sharon has since accompanied me to all subsequent Elio gigs, and, like me, she is blown away by this man's talent.

> *"I met him August 20, 2017, at his motorcycle shop. He was very nice, and I got my picture with him (hence my profile picture), and I shook his hand!! I have a tattoo of him on my chest, across my heart, where he will always be."* **Judy Brandt**, **Millerton NY**.

CHAPTER SEVENTEEN
CARELESS TALK

When Elio Pace agreed to be interviewed for this project, I wanted to make the most of the opportunity.

In my view, the only way to speak to a musician as talented as Elio, to talk about the music of Billy Joel, was sat in front of a piano.

And so I set about trying to find a rehearsal room with a piano to rent for a couple of hours in London. Abbey Road Studios had the perfect room, in historic surroundings…but at a price. There are loads of rooms all over London, but as I discovered, none of them are cheap.

I decided to look further afield, and closer to home for Elio so he didn't have too far to travel. And so by the power of Google, I stumbled across Handel Pianos Limited in Sunningdale, near Ascot.

Using her expert negotiation skills, Sharon contacted Chris Lovell at Handel Pianos who was a little sceptical of my project at first, but agreed to host the interview and make a piano available to us. Free. Of. Charge.

And boy did they come up trumps. We arrived at their showroom ahead of Elio and introduced ourselves to Chris – who was still a little suspicious "….run this book idea by me again". Then Elio showed up and we were directed to their piano storage facility at the rear of their showroom.

Oh. My. God. This was an Aladdin's Cave of pianos. Steinway. C Bechstein. Kemble. Yamaha. In fact, in this converted barn, we were surrounded by half a dozen of the best pianos in the world. To be precise, over a million pounds worth of the best pianos in the world. This was the perfect location to conduct this interview. To talk about, and play the songs of Billy Joel.

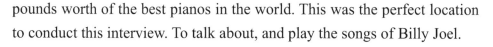

ELIO Pace knew he wasn't sitting opposite a musical genius when I showed him my harmonica skills while he sat at a £70,000 Steinway Concert Grand Piano.

We'd reached a point in the interview when my words were not enough to describe my love of Billy's music, I had to express it.

So, I reached into my briefcase and produced a small blue box containing a £2 harmonica wrapped in tissue paper.

Carefully removing the harmonica and unwrapping it, I sat up proudly in my seat opposite Elio and said "Listen to this".

I'm not sure what Elio was thinking or expecting, but I had been practising this for days before our meeting, and had often impressed (or so I thought), many a dinner party guest with this magical, musical moment.

Those familiar with the song *Piano Man* (put this book down immediately if you're not), will recall the harmonica lick in the chorus; nothing too complicated, just breathing in and out four times and then repeating, hopefully in the right spot, followed by "Sing us a song you're the Piano Man. Sing us a song tonight" etc. When Billy sings this, he's sat at the piano with a Harmonica brace around his neck, and I've always thought it looked a little uncomfortable and awkward. Anyway. Nothing too complicated, right?

Composing myself, I sat up in my chair, all the while gently but purposefully breathing in through my nose, and out through my mouth. I closed my eyes and raised my hand as if to request total silence. I took a deep breath and pressed my lips onto the harmonica, and off I went, huffing and puffing like a 100-a-day smoker trying to blow up a party balloon. World renowned harmonicist (if there is such a word) Toots Thielemans, who actually played on *Leave A Tender Moment Alone* on the *Innocent Man* album, must have turned in his grave.

I sat back in my chair. Closed my eyes and slowly started to bring my breathing down. In through my nose. Out through my mouth. Impressed with my efforts, I opened my eyes and looked down. I noticed a little dribble on the harmonica, but hey. This is Rock n Roll.

There was a moment's silence. I recomposed my gaze and looked up, expecting muted applause from my captive audience.

More silence.

Elio cleared his throat.

"Jon. You've, err, got it upside down mate," he said.

"Eh?" I thought. Does a harmonica have an upside or a downside? Turns out they do.

Elio leaned forward. Took the harmonica from my hand, repositioned it the correct way up and handed it back to me.

"Ah. Right." I cleared my throat. I looked across at Sharon, who had been taking photographs of the interview. She was pinching her nose, trying not to laugh. "Keep The Faith luv", I thought to myself.

"Yer. Thanks Elio. But you get the idea, right?"

"You may not know what you're doing" (harsh), "but with a bit of coaching, you could", he said. YES! I knew it. He wants me in the band.

"I'm a little bit better on the Triangle," I offer.

"There's nothing easy about playing the triangle," says Elio. "Everyone thinks it's an easy instrument to play because we all had a go on one at school. But to actually play one well is a skill, and to say otherwise is a disserve to a lot of percussionists out there."

Alright. I was just saying. Oh never mind.

Elio is one of the nicest people you could ever meet. As mentioned previously, massively talented with an encyclopaedic knowledge of all things Billy. If ever the music of Billy Joel has touched someone so profoundly, then Elio is that person.

For the last five years he has toured the country with his show, The Billy Joel Songbook, selling out wherever he goes (except in Potter's Bar, Hertfordshire, strangely). But getting the gig wasn't easy, and he had to overcome some major showbiz hurdles along the way.

Born in Woking, Surrey in 1968 of Italian parents, he showed early signs of natural musical talent, when, he started to sing and play the piano at the age of four. A similar age when a certain Billy Joel showed the same signs.

Elio went on to train at the Leeds College of Music, an experience he recalls with mixed emotion:

"What was strange about Leeds, was not only was I surrounded by musicians who were not into Billy Joel, they were not into the commercial aspect of music at all. I was meant to be there for three years, but left after two. I was into rock n roll, but was surrounded by people who hated that.

"I'd discovered Billy Joel at this point. His music made utter sense to me. I wasn't impressed by instrumentalists who could play at 100mph.

"A big difference between Billy and me is that classical music was not a big influence in my life. Our upbringing was similar in some ways, but massively different in others. My experience of being a 19 year old could not have been further than what it was for him. It's not that side of Billy that influences me. I guess I had an arrogant self-confidence. Leeds College was the wrong environment for me, but I made some good friends there who were not snobs and liked what I did. I've always been happy being slightly outside of the norm. I was learning Billy Joel's music in the 80s, while everyone else was listening to New Wave". This is starting to sound like a familiar Billy Joel song.

Elio's first big break came in 1988 when, singing and playing his own songs, he reached the final of Bob Says Opportunity Knocks.

For the benefit of younger readers, and those reading this in America, Bob Says Opportunity Knocks is best compared to the global TV talent franchise, X Factor. But back in the 80s, 25 million people were watching this BBC TV phenomenon instead of six million who tune into the X Factor on ITV today.

Elio went on to win. Of course he did. All of a sudden doors were opening everywhere and he regularly appeared on national television alongside TV giants of the era including Terry Wogan, Michael Barrymore and Les Dawson.

At this point, I would ordinarily encourage my American cousins to Google these British TV heavyweights, but, as British readers might be thinking, they may not "get it". I'll leave it up to you.

Loads of musical collaborations followed, including appearing in many theatre productions of the time and also contributing as Musical Director. As well as his theatre commitments, the Elio Pace Band was born in 1993 and the work was never ending.

But always at the back of his mind, Elio had one project that wouldn't go away. He wanted to share his love of Billy Joel because he instinctively knew there was an audience out there for it.

"I'd wanted to do something like the Billy Joel Songbook for over 30 years," said Elio. "And because I knew his music was so special, beautiful and colourful, I couldn't believe nobody else was doing it."

"This was about 1993 and I thought why is nobody singing *Honesty* live anywhere, or *Movin' Out*. I thought this is crazy. These are beautiful songs. I thought, I wanna change that."

So Elio set about getting a proposal together and designed a poster. "I took the idea to a guy very high up in the industry, and he said 'I love this, but you're 20 years too early.'

"Billy was out there doing it and *River Of Dreams* had only just come out. I trusted this industry guy and thought he was right. He knew the business."

And so Elio parked the idea and got on with his life. Then 13 years or so later, he revisited the idea of the Billy Joel Songbook and wrote to 250 theatres all over the country. Just six expressed an interest, while one even thought they might be booking the REAL Billy Joel.

"We realised very quickly it was not worth putting on a tour with only six theatres, and so that was the second knock back. A couple of years later I tried again, contacting people myself. Nothing. Nobody was interested."

I had to find something because I didn't want to go and cruise around the world for the rest of my life performing on ships. I turned down 20 weeks of cruising. I said NO. I need to do something that's going to make me happy and the Billy Joel Songbook was it.

"It sounds glamourous, but it's not fulfilling. They're not there to see you; they're on a cruise and they'll go and see whoever is in the theatre that night."

"I could have accepted many jobs that were well paid and went on for years and years, but I turned them down because I didn't want them," said Elio.

And when Queen legend Brian May approached Elio to help him with a musical project he was working on, he turned him down too. Elio said: "I thought to myself I wish this had come around eight years earlier, but it wasn't the direction I wanted to take, and that took courage."

Elio acknowledges that the music industry is slow to embrace his own compositions, even though he's had his own songs covered around the world, and his Christmas song play-listed on BBC radio. He says the industry can be "so callous" adding that while his appearances as musical director on the BBC Radio show Weekend Wogan was topping the radio charts, record labels were beating a path to his door, but the moment the show folded, fewer opportunities were coming his way.

Elio says: "I had the Billy Joel Songbook within me. This was 2011. Even though it was on the backburner. If I had ended up being a Musical Director for some band, you'd have never seen me doing the Billy Joel Songbook. No one else was doing those songs and I want people to hear them; to not forget Billy"

But then Elio got a break.

On April 15, 1972, Billy Joel and his band – Larry Russell, Rhys Clark and Al Hertzberg - played an hour-long concert at Sigma Studios. The recording of *Captain Jack* from this event received extensive radio play in the Philadelphia area and beyond, long before Billy became widely known, which helped him establish a national following.

In 2013 and then 2014, Elio was invited to fill Billy's shoes and star in five reunion concerts in America with Joel's original 1971-72 touring band, recreating Billy's historic Sigma Sounds live recordings.

More from Larry Russell elsewhere in this book.

Elio explains: "Sony were going to put out the recording of the 1972 show remixed and remastered. They (Sony) had been in contact with Larry Russell and Rhys about it. Al Hertzberg wasn't available at the time due to illness, so they asked Don Evans to fill the guitar slot. Don had played on *Cold Spring Harbor* and toured with Billy in the early 70s.

"They needed a "Billy" because they (Sony) got wind that Billy wasn't going to be "Billy" for this reunion. He didn't want to go back. And so Larry Russell, who was running the whole thing asked a musician called David

Clark to front the group. David was busy with his own band and his own thing, so they went looking for another guy, and that's when I got the call.

"I have to thank the Billy Joel Completely Retold Facebook page (more on this later) for this. The site is run by a guy called Mike Stutz (more on him later too) who has been an avid Billy Joel collector for many years.

"So it was via the Retold website that I got a message from Larry Russell saying "can we talk" and that's how that came about. It was massively exciting," says Elio.

It was following on from the success of these shows that, in 2014, the Billy Joel Songbook finally grew arms and legs.

"We approached a booking agent called Barry Collins and we put the 70 date tour together. I was the first. I'm proud to admit that. We were the first in the world to ever tour a Billy Joel show around the nation constantly. Not do one or two gigs. But a big tour. And then do it the next year and the year after that."

Advertising the shows is still not financially viable for Elio: "To place an ad in a national paper is £65k and I can't afford to do that, so it's all about word of mouth. Without Facebook, I think I would have had to stop after about the first half a year.

"For me singing Billy's songs live is fulfilling a life-long ambition. And to see the audience reaction as I imagined it to be is incredible.

"A lot of people may think "he's had to get his sold out tour via someone else's genius", and I don't mind that.

"If I appeared on Jools Holland's show for just one song, my ticket sales would double overnight. Isn't it funny it takes that? If Jools Holland says it's good, then it must be. That's the world we live in. What that says to me is "Do it all yourself, mate", so it doesn't get me down.

"I'll continue to do what I do, as long as it is at a high level. I'm going to make another album of Billy's rare songs – which will be the first time a lot of people will have heard these songs – then after that I'm going to write another album of my own material."

When Elio talks of playing at a "high level", he's not exaggerating. His band are top notch and Elio puts EVERYTHING he's got into his performance.

"The last tour was 50 dates and I was exhausted. Really exhausted. And the last third of the tour I really started to feel it. It's tough. But if you do something you love, it isn't a job. It's not work, is it?"

In the show, Elio talks passionately about his "Billy Joel moment". The moment that Billy's music touched his life and made him change direction.

For me, that moment was hearing "*Scenes From An Italian Restaurant*", and falling in love with the romance of Brenda and Eddie.

For Elio, his song was "*This Night*", a track from 1983's *An Innocent Man* album. In the show he says how one line from that song moved him like no other song.

"*An Innocent Man*, is probably overall my favourite album," says Elio. *This Night* was my defining moment. It's just the way he sang it. The sound of his voice on that line and being able to deliver in a style that really spoke to me.

"I didn't know *Big Shot*, or *Movin' Out* or *Nylon Curtain* at this point. I couldn't believe my luck with this album. I couldn't believe what I was hearing. It's my favourite album. It's romantic. It's colourful. It's rock n roll."

Throughout Elio's show, he imparts his extensive knowledge of Billy's songs and music, telling true stories, funny stories and romantic stories along the way.

"I really feel that to love Billy Joel is to be part of a "club" that you "get". His music touches people in different ways. I don't think McCartney has it. Springsteen doesn't have it. I can't think of another musician who touches people with their music and lyrics in the same way. For me as a musician, I judge everything else by him."

And so, as we're sat at the piano together, our one hour interview becomes two, then three. But hang on, we've booked a table at Pizza Express to continue the conversation: "Phone them up and tell them we'll be late. There's no point in rushing this," says Elio.

Suits me. And so we talk about the Billy Joel tracks that shaped our lives. We agree on some: The Stranger's *She's Always A Woman* and 52nd Street's *Until The Night*, but disagree on others: The Stranger's *Vienna* ("I will admit to not really understanding what the hell Vienna is all about" says Elio), and from the same album, *Everybody Has A Dream*.

My own Billy Joel knowledge is questioned; when I talk about the song *Streetlife Serenade*, I'm reminded the track is actually called *Streetlife SerenadER*, and the album is *Streetlife Serenade*. The line from *Say Goodbye To Hollywood* which I recite as "Johnny's driving through the city tonight…." "Actually, Jon. It's Bobby. Not Johnny," says Elio.

But it's all good banter, with Elio demonstrating the songs along the way; playing the frantic opening to *Angry Young Man* at full speed, then slowing it down, before speeding it up again; *Movin Out, Summer Highland Falls*. The beauty of the melody even before the powerful lyrics that touch a chord with millions – I'll say that again, MILLIONS – of people ALL. AROUND. THE. WORLD.

I'm in Billy Joel heaven, and Elio looks like he's having a ball too. Oh how I wish I could play the piano.

I ask Elio to teach me the piano rift to *Movin' Out*, using my left hand. I try but find it hard keeping the rhythm: "You couldn't just 'do it', unless you were innately talented," says Elio as he shows off his innate talent.

"Howabout showing me the opening rift to *Only The Good Die Young* then," I ask like a wide eyed schoolboy in a sweetshop. "Forget it," comes Elio's withering reply. Ok, I'll leave it to the professionals.

And so nearly four hours after we started, the official interview comes to a close and we head over the road to Pizza Express.

I leave the tape recorder running, and the talk turns away from Billy and onto more personal stuff.

So. To sum up. Can Elio describe the genius of Billy Joel in one sentence?: "I think he is the most over-qualified rock star there has ever been."

What a day we've had. Talking. Laughing. Playing. Singing. All of our favourite Billy Joel songs. Sharon's been on hand to record the magical occasion – some of it on video. And as we say our goodbyes, we feel we have made a friend. Someone who "gets it". Someone so talented. So down to earth, giving his time and talent for nothing to help me write this book. Thanks Elio.

CHAPTER EIGHTEEN
DAVID BROWN

Not content with simply performing the Billy Joel Songbook, Elio decided to take things up a notch, stealing the mark on even the best of the best Billy Joel tribute acts in the United States.

In May 2018, Elio launched the Albums Tour, playing Glass Houses and An Innocent Man in their entirety, not only with his usual band, but with a very special guest.

As things went from national to International for Billy in the late 70s following the success of The Stranger, Billy needed a new lead guitarist. And so the word went out and Billy's bass player at the time and band leader, Doug Stegmeyer enlisted the help of a new kid on the block who had been making a name for himself around New York.

Toward the end of the 52nd Street sessions, enter David Brown, described as one of the most unique guitarists in pop music history.

With his laid back approach, dry sense of humour and skill, David quickly became a mainstay of the Billy Joel Band, recording platinum-selling albums and touring the world over with Billy.

Tiring from the rigours of touring the world, David decided to call it a day with the Billy Joel Band and went on to work with the likes of Paul McCartney and Simon and Garfunkel.

And so when Elio was looking for a twist to his albums show concept, he made the tentative approach to David, and was delighted when he said YES.

"This is the guy who, as a young man, I watched and admired from afar playing lead guitar in Billy Joel's band during my very first Billy Joel live concert in May 1990," said Elio.

"I was absolutely transfixed and blown away by what I was seeing and hearing and never in a million years would I have imagined that the same David Brown would one day fly over from the USA especially to play in my band".

And this wasn't just for one show, but a 10 date tour playing, track by track, Glass Houses and An Innocent Man. Records that David actually played on for the original recordings.

"This is David's first international tour and first visit to the UK since he left Billy's band in 1991," he added.

Mrs B and I were fortunate enough to attend two of these ground-breaking shows. Firstly at The Stables in Milton Keynes and then a week later in London's Leicester Square.

The transformation of David from the MK gig, where he was humble and shy, to the London gig where he transfixed the audience with tales of recording these great songs with the man himself was lovely to see.

Not one for hogging the limelight, David was initially happy to take very much a back seat in the proceedings, looking slightly uncomfortable as the larger than life Elio tried expertly to tease him out of his shell.

In the show program, David says: "Although the material you will hear tonight was recorded an estimated 38 years ago, another hope is that the joy and spirit still ring true.

"I'm surely a different player now than so long ago, but that is part of the fun. Music is eternal and boundless. There is room for emotion, personality and interpretation with every piece at any time.

"And this is what I loved in learning about Elio. He puts himself into this music to express his interpretation with his own personality," said David.

By the time of that second gig David was cracking jokes and even participating in a Q&A with members of the audience keen to hear those tales and titbits of times gone by. Almost 40 years, in fact.

For a fan like myself, this was Billy Joel gold. And Elio had pulled it off with quite possibly the most memorable Billy Joel show ever.

It was so good, Elio, damn him, has got me questioning my inner Billy Joel self. Could Elio's shows be better than the real thing? Of course Elio *isn't* (nor claims to be!) the real thing, but his live shows, in intimate theatres with a brilliant band and sound system, are actually a better audience experience than sitting at the back of a massive arena or stadium with poor and often distorted sound and no view.

Of course, part of the experience is being in the same "room" as Billy himself, but for fans of the music, many would argue that Elio is all round better value for money. And this is a difficult thing for me to say.

Following on from the success of this ten date tour, a further "albums" show featuring David has been scheduled for October 2019 where The Stranger and Storm Front will be played in their entirety. Brilliant.

CHAPTER NINETEEN

SCENES FROM THE VILLAGE GREEN – OCTOBER 2018

"Of all of the cabs, in all of Hicksville, you hadda get into mine"

During an earlier trip to Long Island two years ago, we hopped in a taxi at Hicksville Railroad Station to drive us two miles to the Hicksville Econo Lodge.

As we pulled up outside the motel, I asked the driver: "So. Tell me. Have you had anyone famous in the back of your cab?"

"Nah", came the reply.

"Not even Billy Joel? I hear he's from round these parts," I said.

The cab screeched to a halt outside reception. The driver spun around and said: "You like Billy Joel?"

And so started a 30 minute conversation about the man, his music and his life around Hicksville. Luckily the meter had stopped running.

Turns out our taxi driver, John Marchut, who has lived in the area all his life, is the creator and owner of the world's most visited fan website called mylifebillyjoel.com. If you don't believe me, Google "popular Billy Joel websites" and it is likely to be either number one or two on the search return.

Although this book was just an idea at the time, I remembered the site, and our taxi driver's name because I knew that having him contribute to this book would be a unique touch. And after all, of all the taxis on Long Island, what were the chances of me getting in that cab that day?

And so two years and a few emails later, at 11am on a bright 2018 October Sunday morning, Sharon and I are stood outside the Hicksville Railroad branch of Dunkin' Donuts waiting to see John again.

I spotted John walking toward us. He was wearing a bright blue baseball cap, jeans and treasured Billy Joel t-shirt. John crossed the street and greeted us with the biggest, most genuine smile I have ever seen, and will never forget. Aged 64, he looks 15 years younger, and has a sprightly spring in his step.

"This is so crazy," he said. "I can't believe this is happening. It's so lovely to see you guys again. I can't believe the chances of you getting in my cab two years ago."

A Hicksville taxi driver for almost 40 years, if John takes a day off, he doesn't get paid. And John had taken the day off especially to spend time with us. But at least he wouldn't have to do the driving.

We deliberately upgraded our rental car because we knew John would be joining us and pointing out all the relevant Billy Joel sites, and the three of us couldn't sit cramped in a two door economy heap of junk. So, it had to be a Chevy!

Re-introductions over, John hopped in the passenger seat in the front while Sharon got comfortable in the back.

"I've prepared an itinerary for us," said John, carefully removing a hand-written list of places to visit, which he had thoughtfully placed in a plastic envelope in case of rain.

And so we were off. First stop, 20 Meeting Lane. Childhood home of Billy Joel. "Billy never liked to boast about being from Hicksville," explained John. "For years he would tell people he was from Levittown, which is a mile from here. It made him sound better, rather than from HICKSville. He hated that".

Sharon and I had visited the Meeting Lane address previously, but the current owner has painted out the "20" on her mailbox, apparently sick and tired of Billy Joel fans walking over her front yard and indiscriminately taking photos.

"There's the bedroom window he used to climb out to go to the Village Green," said John as he pointed his enormous camera at the house. "You know the song *Half A Mile Away*, well that was what he was referring to."

A short drive around the corner is the Village Green. Made famous in the song *Scenes From An Italian Restaurant*, and again, a place Sharon and I had visited before. But this time, we had an expert with us.

"You see that laundromat over there? That's where Billy would sleep as a kid if he was too drunk to go home. He'd go to the bar next door, which used to be called "Fantastics" with his friends and skip school the next day."

Back in the car and just around the corner, Hicksville High School, where Billy famously didn't graduate from until 1992.

Leaving Hicksville behind us, we head North and toward Oyster Bay. Along the way John tells us what life was like growing up on Long Island. We head through John's childhood neighbourhood in Syosset and take a short detour to drive past the family home. A neat and large house on a substantial plot. "We had a pretty good middle class upbringing", said John, the eldest of four children. "My parents lived in this house from 1960 right up until 2000"

We paused briefly outside the house, and I took a moment to look closely at John. Tears briefly filled his eyes. And we drove off.

Still headed toward Oyster Bay and we pass a restaurant called The George Martin 1989. No connection that I could tell to the famous Beatles producer.

As we drove by, pointing at the restaurant, John said: "You see that place there. It used to be called Heads & Tails and was a popular joint. That's where I bought Billy a beer."

John went on to explain: "It was the summer of 1977 and I went there with my girlfriend at the time. The place was packed, noisy and smoky, but sitting in a booth on his own was Billy Joel.

"He wasn't the big star he is now, but I knew him from the other bands he had played with in the local area. We went right over to him and I asked if we could join him. He said "Sure". We got chatting and it turned out he was taking a break from completing his fifth solo album – The Stranger.

"As we finished our first round of Budweiser's, I offered to get the second round and while I was at the bar, my girlfriend got his autograph." John now has that autograph. One of two in his personal collection.

And as our journey continued, the stories kept coming. John explained how he dated Mary Sue Weber, the sister of Billy's first wife Elizabeth Weber. He told how they used to hang out with Doug Stegmeyer, who lived just four blocks away from John's house. He told how they would smoke pot and get high. Doug went on to become Billy's bass player on nearly all of his biggest albums.

Tragically Doug took his own life soon after Billy took a break from touring. "Doug lived a lavish lifestyle in those days," said John. "Big house. Flash car. Billy paid him well, and when the pay checks stopped coming, he could no longer afford the lifestyle."

There are many theories amongst fans and other former band members as to the reasons why Doug took his own life in August 1995. Ultimately only one person knows the answer why, and that is Doug himself.

The journey continued and soon we are in Oyster Bay, the town immortalised in the song *The Ballad of Billy The Kid.*

We head straight to 20th Century Cycles, the showroom in the town where Billy now keeps, and proudly displays, his incredible collection of around 100 motorbikes. Billy graciously opens the showroom to his fans and the public at weekends. There's no charge to look around and none of the bikes are for sale.

Stepping into the showroom is like stepping back into the fifties. The smell of petrol, or gas as the Americans say, adds to the atmosphere as you examine this amazing collection.

But the bikes aren't simply museum pieces to be admired, all are fully fuelled, charged and ready to ride off the minute Billy turns up for a bike.

John talks to me as we admire the collection: "The best time to catch Billy is when he comes here to change his bike over. He'll take a bike out for a week or so, then bring it back and swap it for another one.

"I've calculated that the best time to be here is between 11am and 2.30pm. That's when he's likely to show." No luck today.

Chatting to John is so easy. His love of everything Billy. Everything Long Island, is plain to see and his enthusiasm infectious. He's great company.

It's clear Billy won't be showing up today, so, on the recommendation of John, we head to Taby's, a famous Oyster Bay diner and reportedly the place Billy turned up at the morning after his latest marriage to collect his favourite take out lunch.

John tucked into a deluxe Taby burger, while Sharon and I shared a tuna melt with fries, our body's not having adjusted to the time difference, having arrived in New York a day ealier. The conversation, and the laughter, never stopped for a minute. We were having the time of our lives.

Back on the road and John took us to Billy's home, a $30+ million dollar mansion in a private community in Centre Island just five miles away. This tiny enclave – with its own Police Department, boasts dream houses not just of incredible proportions, but also an incredible location. We pause briefly for a photo of Billy's gates before visiting his former homes in Cove Neck and Lloyd Neck, all within a short distance of each other – if travelling by boat. We catch a glimpse of his famous Glass House home, as featured on the cover of the *Glass Houses* album.

With the sun still shining, we head to the wealthy hamlet of Cold Spring Harbor, and the park that has been dedicated to Billy Joel.

Billy's first solo album, famously mastered at the wrong speed, was named *Cold Spring Harbor*. Released in November 1971, the cover, designed by Ruby Mazur, features Billy with moustache, looking pensive. The album featured stand out tracks, *She's Got A Way*, *Everybody Loves You Now* and *Falling Of The Rain*.

The Billy Joel Cold Spring Harbor Park was officially dedicated on July 17, 1991 and a brass plaque, embedded in a rock, was unveiled. The ceremony was attended by local dignitaries, Billy Joel and, er, his mom, Rosalind. The absence of Christie Brinkley was seen by many to be an indicator that things weren't going too well in the marriage department at the time.

We stand and pause for a while in the sunshine looking out over the harbour. John reflects about how great life – and living, is. John is thoughtful and sincere about everything he says. He has a deep sense of pride, not just for Billy Joel, but for Long Island in general. He explains, with a slightly angry tone, that there used to be a blue sign dedicating the park to Billy, but that it had been stolen. He pointed out the area where former Beatle John Lennon once lived.

Our journey continues through the town of Huntington where we stop for a cool drink and stroll around town, before heading for the final destination of the day.

We return to Syosset, and the former location of the Italian Restaurant, Christiano's.

John explained that back in the late sixties, seventies and eighties, Christiano's was THE place to be seen.

"The original owners name was Jimmy Christiano," said John. "Billy patronised this restaurant for decades. If you grew up in Syosset, you went to Christiano's to drink, eat great Italian food and to be seen. I personally saw Billy Joel in that restaurant many times. In fact, I have a beer mat that Billy signed for me from there.

John continued: "Although Billy grew up in Hicksville, he started to hang out in Syosset. This is where he met the members of The Hassles before he joined the band. They were ALL from Syosset. And this is where Billy met his first wife, his manager, his hair stylist and Doug Stegmeyer.

"Billy claims in an interview that 'Italian Restaurant' wasn't about Christiano's and it was some other place in New York City, which is not true. The first time he ever played 'Italian Restaurant' he dedicated the song to Christiano's!

"And later on in his life, he wined and dined Christie Brinkley there! Anyway, Jimmy and Billy had a falling out over some kind of disagreement, and Billy wouldn't plug Christiano's anymore. If Billy Joel gets angry and mad at you, you are shut out of his life. Just ask Liberty DeVitto!

"This is why I know so much about Billy Joel, because all the people he surrounded himself with back in the late 60s and early 70s were all from Syosset, and I knew them all!"

And so there you are, dear readers, the reason why I was so honoured that John Marchut agreed to be a part of this book. He was there, and his story has never been shared.

Now a Chinese restaurant and take away, Sharon and I had been lucky enough to visit the iconic Christiano's before it was sold. Full details of that visit are outlined earlier in the book.

Never before published photos of Billy in concert at the MGM Grand, Las Vegas, November 2007.

Unusually Billy is wearing jeans and a t-shirt. Nowadays he feels more comfortable performing in a designer suit.

Photos: Jon Brett

Above: Is it or isn't it? Thought by many to be the inspiration for Scenes From An Italian Restaurant, Christiano's in Syosset. Now a Chinese restaurant.

Photo credit: John Marchut

Left: Sharon outside Billy's Sag Harbor residence.

Above left: "What the f**k?" Debbielou Houdek shares her Billy Joel Sag Harbor secrets with us. Above and inset: Cold Spring Harbor Park, dedicated to Billy Joel.

Left: Coolest Cabbie in Hicksville, our friend and owner of mylifebillyjoel. com, John Marchut.

Left: Liberty DeVitto

Left: David Clark after lunch. Notice the street sign he's stood under.

Right: David Clark in action.

Photo: Kevin Mocker

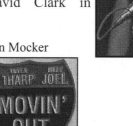

Left and Right: Captain Broadway. Michael Cavanaugh, original star of Movin' Out.

Photos: Supplied

Left: Shock Jock Eric Skjeveland.

Right: Tony Walker.

Below: Sallie O'Neill. Hicksville based Govs Radio trio who kindly invited me on their show to talk about the book.

Above: Elio Pace demonstrates his love of Billy's music to me.
Photo: Sharon Brett

Below left: Elio Pace on stage at The Stables in the UK with Billy's former lead guitarist, David Brown.
Photo: Jon Brett

Below right: Signed programme. Reproduced with permission.

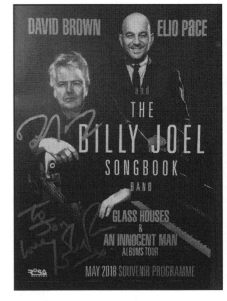

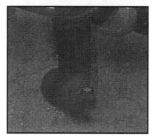

Engineer (Ugg!) boots, leather jackets and tight blue jeans. Is it Billy or Eddie at his bike shop in Oyster Bay?

Billy at his bike shop, 20th Century Cycles.

Photos: Jon Brett

This is the moment Sharon met Billy, and uttered those immortal words: "Shall I hold your helmet?" Blushing, he handed it over and signed an autograph joking "That'll be $8.50 please"

CHAPTER TWENTY

LORDS OF 52ND STREET

They're not a tribute act, they're the real deal.

Drummer Liberty DeVitto, guitarist Russell Javors, saxophonist Richie Cannata and, posthumously, bass player Doug Stegmeyer, made up The Lords of 52nd Street - the musicians who appeared on most of Billy's top charting albums from Turnstiles onwards.

It was actually producer Phil Ramone and Billy himself who coined the phrase "The Lords Of 52nd Street" to describe the band, based on the location of the former CBS studios.

Much has already been written about this group of, some might say, dispirited New Yorkers who, one by one, were "let go" from the Billy Joel band at one time or another. Doug, in somewhat tragic circumstances.

It was in 2014 that the surviving members of The Lords reunited after being inducted into the Long Island Music Hall of Fame. And almost 30 years after last playing together, in 2016, decided to return to live performance.

I would have been keen to get the inside track from this disaffected group. I wanted to spend some quality time with Liberty DeVitto and get beyond the bitterness and the soundbites and really try to feel their pain objectively.

Before flying to New York on my most recent trip, I reached out to Liberty, explained my project and invited him to take part. Initially he responded saying: "I'm sorry, but due to the past lawsuit, I am unable to participate."

Not realising it appeared there was some form of gagging or non-disclosure order in place, I tried a different approach, wanting to concentrate simply on the life of Liberty, but still I was knocked back.

Shortly after I returned to the UK, I noticed Liberty had organised a drum workshop in Hicksville where he would be talking drums…and about his life on the road with Billy Joel. Mmmm. Okay.

I truly felt it was a shame that he was unwilling to meet with me. However, the relationship between Liberty and Billy has been well documented - Liberty alleged that Billy had failed to pay him undisclosed royalties based on sales of 11 albums recorded between 1975 and 1990. The two former friends settled out of court in 2010.

I knew this project would survive without repeating the same old arguments.

And so I thought you wouldn't be hearing too much more about them in this book…mainly because Liberty DeVitto declined – graciously – my invitation to take part. In fact, of all the people I had approached to take part in this project, Liberty was the only person to say no.

Nevertheless, despite the bitterness that now exists, I did still think I might be able to squeeze a few nostalgic memories about the "good old days" out of Liberty, but it wasn't to be. Or so I thought.

In January 2019, a podcast interview with Liberty was made available on the internet, and in it, he talks freely about life on the road with Billy Joel, and life afterwards.

Perhaps Liberty had softened, and would now consider speaking to me, and so I made a third and final approach, and I'm pleased to say that Liberty agreed to answer some questions via email.

This is never my preferred method of interview. So much more can be gained face to face, or via Skype. It's impossible to convey a sense of feeling or emotion, or pick up on facial expressions or other body language indicators with a series of typed questions and answers.

I also wanted to avoid asking the same old questions, getting the same old answers. In my experience, it's only through conversation that the whole story can be heard, and felt.

With limited questions, and sensing only a limited willingness to take part, I had to make the best of what was being offered. And while the words you read are Liberty's replies, I feel a deeper, richer, story remains unwritten.

Liberty was with Billy through the glory years. What personal highlights can he recall? "There were so many memorable highlights over the 30 years. I saw Billy go from a cult following to world domination.

"Two highlights have got to be playing in the Soviet Union, and Havana, Cuba. A low point was after 9/11. Billy lost it at Madison Square Garden. We all did."

So what was it like touring the world over, selling out wherever the band went?: "I loved touring. I love hotels. You wake up around 10am and go downstairs and when you get back to your room the bed is made and dirty towels are picked up and replaced with new ones.

"I did miss my daughters growing up. That was tough. There were no cell phones like today."

The basis of the lawsuit was that Liberty's creative input had not been recognised, or somehow overlooked. How does that make him feel today?: "If you're talking overlooked by other drummers, then I don't really care. 150 million albums sold can't be wrong. I play what suits the song. I'm not out to impress anyone."

How does Liberty feel about the success of the Lords Of 52nd Street? "Hey. We were a bunch of friends doing what we loved to do. If we made money at it, then great. I never dreamed it would be so huge. We really have to thank Classic Radio for playing that shit to death!"

Is the feud with Billy over? Will you guys be having lunch together anytime soon? "I don't think it will ever be over. We are both stubborn people. So I guess lunch is out of the question!"

If invited, would you go back on the road with Billy?: "I would never go on the road with him again."

Have you been to any of Billy's shows recently?: "I have not been to any shows, but I have seen some videos on Youtube. It irks me that in the beginning it was said we parted ways due to musical difference. Bullshit. The guy who is playing now, is playing all the parts that I created."

Finally, can you tell us something about Billy Joel that no-one else knows? "Brussel sprouts are his favourite vegetable."

I can't be certain the last answer is 100 per cent genuine, but I think Liberty has been pretty honest with the others.

And so while Liberty, Richie and Russell make up The Lords, it is pianist and vocalist David Clark who's in the driving seat during shows as far as filling in for Billy goes.

I thought it would be appropriate to meet up with David at Rosie O'Grady's bar and restaurant on, er, 52nd Street in New York to talk about his love of all things Billy, and getting the gig as the Piano Man himself when playing live with The Lords of 52nd Street.

A native of Hempstead, Long Island, a young David was heavily influenced by his father who had made a successful career as a musician on the weddings and corporate circuit.

Following in his father's footsteps, he took up the piano aged just eight, and says his first exposure to Billy Joel was in 1977, aged 10, when he heard *Just The Way You Are* for the first time.

"I knew at that moment what I wanted to be, and I wanted to be like him," David told me over a fish and chip lunch.

"It was that song and that album that changed the way I played and studied piano. I didn't like the way I was being taught, so I modelled my singing and playing after him because of The Stranger."

Over the coming months, David would use his allowance to purchase the other Billy Joel albums already available including Cold Spring Harbor and Piano Man.

"But it was the Songs In The Attic album that made me feel differently about those songs," explains David. "Growing up on Long Island I became aware of how big Billy was going to be. At the time, I didn't realise he was actually from Long Island".

Despite listing Star Wars, Star Trek and baseball as the other great influences in his life, David decided, like his father before him, to embark on a career in music.

And so in 2011, and bearing more than just a passing resemblance to a certain Mr Joel, David launched his own Billy Joel tribute band, called Songs In The Attic.

But on Long Island, Mike DelGuidice's Big Shot had pretty much cornered the market in Billy Joel tribute shows.

"I've known Mike for a long time. He's one of my favourite singers. He's a very pure, clean, powerful vocalist.

"Big Shot was already established. I didn't want to challenge that, but I launched Songs In The Attic for me. I just wanted to have fun playing that music. If I get gigs, great. If I don't, I die in six months.

"That didn't happen. I didn't think it was going to catch on, but it did. I was shocked to find there was room for it. I thought I'd do a couple of shows and it would be over, but we were better received than I thought," said David.

Word was spreading of David's skill at performing the music of Billy Joel, and this led to a phone call from Billy's original touring bass player, Larry Russell, asking him to be a "Billy" for the Sigma Studio reunion.

"If there was no Songs In The Attic, there would have been no Sigma. And if there had been no Sigma, there would have been no Lords of 52nd Street," says David.

"Originally Larry wanted me and Mike DelGuidice to do Sigma, but Mike couldn't and I was reluctant to take on the whole show, and that's when Elio Pace got involved. Elio was amazing and we couldn't have done the shows without him."

And a year later – in 2014, David received another phone call, this time from The Lords of 52nd Street asking him to be their Piano Man when they played at their induction to the Long Island Music Hall of Fame.

"Let's be honest. It's okay to say I wasn't the first call. The first call is always going to be to Mike DelGuidice, but at that point, he was in Billy's band. So I don't take any shame in the fact that I was the second call, but I got the call, and that means a lot to me. I feel I was being taken seriously."

Following the success of the Hall Of Fame reunion, The Lords decided to make it a regular thing, and they wanted to keep David part of the team.

Does David pick up on any of the resentment band members may feel toward Billy?: "There definitely is some resentment. I don't feel weird about it because it is 'on the record'. But I can tell you that when we're playing, you would never guess they were upset about anything.

"They are mostly very light-hearted, funny guys. Liberty is hysterical and Richie and I like to talk about dogs. They do reminisce about the old days, and there are lots of stories.

"There's a long history there and they've known each other a long time.

There are certain questions I don't ask. What they do with honouring Doug is really good. I have my own opinions about how they all feel about Doug, but I don't blame Billy for that.

"My job with The Lords is to do it the way they want me to do it. They've hired me to be their singer. I'm singing, but I'm not the front guy, Richie Cannata is.

"I'll do it for as long as I'm available, but I also have my own show and my own business. But as long as I'm available and they want me and I want to do it, I'll do it. I love doing it.

"Growing up as a teenager, you went to see original bands. Now I think the music scene is driven by covers bands and tribute bands. There's a lot of us, but The Lords is something very different. Very special and it's fun. I mean, how do you not get excited?" said David.

Does this continued interest in Billy Joel surprise David?: "When I go to the Garden I see such a mixed age group of people. You see 10, 12, 13 year olds along with 60 and 70 year olds and everything in-between.

"That is quite a statement about a guy who has not released a lick of new material since 1993, so I think he's going to be relevant for a long time when others have gone. I love it that he is still so relevant," says David.

And while David's band Songs In The Attic and The Lords Of 52nd Street continue to bring the music of Billy Joel to new generations, those shows at Madison Square Garden will continue to sell and sell.

CHAPTER TWENTY ONE
NO FANS LAND

Any Billy Joel event in the UK is a rare thing. He seems to average playing in the UK every two to five years – which is just as well because this is how long it takes to save up for a pair of tickets.

Prior to Billy's most recent UK gig at Old Trafford football ground in Manchester in June 2018 (£105 per ticket), he played at London's Wembley Stadium on 10 September 2016 (£95 per ticket) – a cold, rainy September evening and before that, his most intimate London gig to date at Hammersmith Apollo on Tuesday November 5, 2013 (£65 per ticket).

The Hammersmith Apollo opened in 1932, is a Grade II* listed building built in the Art Deco style and has a fascinating history. The history would have really appealed to Billy who has a love of the subject.

Most notably, Buddy Holly performed two shows at the venue in 1958 – his last ever UK shows.

Between late 1964 and early 1965, The Beatles played an incredible 38 shows over 21 nights and in 1966 Johnny Cash played there too.

Of Billy's more recent contemporaries, in 1973 the venue hosted David Bowie; 1974 Elton John; 1975 Bruce Springsteen; it's a rock n roll who's who and this is just the seventies. With a capacity of around 4,000, this is the best venue to see a concert by Billy Joel.

Of course I managed to bag a couple of standing tickets for the Hammersmith gig which meant a good view down at the front.

Contrast this with Old Trafford.

Old Trafford is the largest club football stadium in the United Kingdom and is the 11th largest stadium in Europe with a capacity of 70,000 – 80,000 people, depending on the event.

Home to the Manchester United football team (that's soccer for my American readers), the venue was nicknamed the Theatre Of Dreams by former Manchester United player Sir Bobby Charlton. He's obviously never been to a concert there. More of that later.

Manchester (the United Kingdom version, not the American cities of the same name) is situated in Northern England with a wide, varied and traditional history dating back hundreds of years which has rendered the city nowadays a dump.

Okay. Okay. So maybe I'm being a bit harsh. But why on God's Earth did Billy think it would be a good idea to play his only UK gig in 2018 there??

Wembley Stadium may not have been quite sold out when he played there in 2016, and so maybe his team thought it would be a good idea to soak up a few extra British Pounds by playing a gig "Oop North" (again, American readers will perhaps not understand the term used here, but it is English for "up north").

Regardless of this, it didn't stop me reaching deep into my pockets and tackling the Ticketshyster website as soon as tickets were made available in October 2017 – eight months before the concert. But I'm sure my money will be well looked after.

Once again, unless you're Billy, the band, the box office manager or the Mafia, you're never gonna get a good seat at a venue like this. And of course, Ticketshyster withhold the best seats, selling them at an outrageous premium which is way beyond the means of most fans. I don't actually *know* that's what happens to the good tickets, I'm guessing. But whatever happens, fans miss out on the best seats unless they're super rich.

And there's always the gamble – do I get the "best seats" being offered at the time the tickets go on sale, or hold out until a few weeks before the gig when "great production seats now available" ads might appear in National newspapers which really pisses you off if you tried to get in early.

Anyway. After many hours spent online trying to order tickets, and telling the ticket selling robot that I'M not a robot, I manage to buy what I think are the best seats I'm going to get: Entrance S20; block Sth123; row 5; seats 191 and 192. This is a BIG venue.

Of course I purchased the tickets based on the seating plan which is barely visible to anyone over the age of 25 using a computer and the £105 per ticket price was, of course, just the starting point. Let's add in the rip off £12 a ticket "Service Charge" (thanks Ticketshyster) and the final basket for tickets alone is a hefty £234.

And so the spending begins, and this rapidly turns out to be my most expensive Billy concert to date.

Let's factor in return Virgin train fares from my home city Milton Keynes (approx. £160) and a hotel for the weekend - £150 (more about THAT later), plus food and other incidentals and the Brett bank account has taken a hefty £500 hit. This had better be a bloody good concert.

And as the big day approaches, I make enquiries for two nights' hotel accommodation. I quickly discover Manchester is an expensive place to stay, particularly on a Billy Joel weekend.

I scour Hotels.com. Booking.com and even that waste of time Trivago.com and the best I can come up with is the Rembrandt Hotel, which is nothing more than a crap "room above a pub". Only it was even worse than that.

Having arrived at Manchester Piccadilly station, it was a short 7 minute walk to the Rembrandt which, unbeknown to me, wasn't just in the heart of Manchester's Gay Village, it was the CENTRE of the Gay Village. The closer we got to the "hotel", the more camp it was becoming; rainbow flags, drag queens and drug dealers on every corner. This was like a scene from *Captain Jack*.

The Rembrandt Hotel is a pub on the ground floor; Manchester's most popular gay 80's disco – The Tropicana - on the first floor, and six of the seediest, tiniest rooms on the second floor. The guy who seemed to be running the joint – all 5ft2ins of him skipped and shimmied over to us like an extra from West Side Story and said: "Welcome to the Rem." Rapid blinking of eyes. "I hope you're not expecting much. But you've got the best room in the place. By the way, the disco usually finishes around 5 or 6am. Just so's you know."

And so we went upstairs to our room. I opened the curtain expecting a panoramic view over the City, but was greeted with a brick wall less than a foot away, and a roosting pigeon staring back at me. The mattress was barely a few inches off the floor, and a separate cubical barely large enough for a toilet and shower. And when you sat on the toilet, it wasn't even possible to shut the door. The lighting was dim, but bright enough to make out the pubic hairs in the shower tray.

Oh boy, was I getting daggers from Mrs B or what? She was expecting at least a Travelodge, or Holiday Inn Express. This was nothing better than a working men's hostel in the seediest part of town with a dodgy lock on the door.

I had to remain focused. The reason we were here was to see Billy. And nothing (or so we thought) was going to ruin that. I quickly suggested we leave our bags, head into the city for coffee before making our way to Old Trafford to soak up the atmosphere, buy a few souvenirs and chow down on a giant stadium burger with fried onions.

Manchester itself was heaving. There were events on all over the city – hence the high price and shortage of hotel rooms, including a gig that night by Lionel Ritchie.

As we tip toed over the drunks, did our best to avoid the homeless beggars in every run down and boarded up shop doorway, dodge the drug dealers and avoid eye contact with the gang members, I quickly formed the opinion Manchester wasn't a city for us.

Old Trafford isn't in the city centre. It's a tram ride away. So we got the tram and got off where told. Then we took shelter as the rain started to pour…and pour…and pour.

Fortunately we were near a pub and I was able to pay £10 for two drinks. If you're reading this book in the year 2025, this might sound quite a reasonable price. But in 2018, it ain't. Trust me.

And then we walked to Old Trafford. And walked. And walked. And bloody walked. It was miles away, but at least it stopped raining. We got there, managed to find the right entrance and queued. And queued. And bloody queued. The gates opened almost an hour late.

Tempting as it was to buy a burger outside the venue, we decided to wait and see what the catering options were like once inside. Certainly at Wembley Stadium there was plenty of choice. And having previously checked the Old Trafford website, it assured me food was available inside.

Only it wasn't. Well, unless you class a tasteless hotdog in a stale roll dinner, this was as good as it was going to get. Sharon asked if we could "upgrade" to onions, only to be told there were no onions, but "free" ketchup was available behind us…in a mostly empty plastic bottle…with more ketchup running down the OUTSIDE than in it. I forget how much I was charged for them. Well. I say "forget", but just don't want to think about it. This was as bad as it could be. Surely?

Unable to physically consume the majority of the hot dog, we give up and bin it, and decide to buy a bottle of water to restore some moisture to our mouths.

Meanwhile, the atmosphere at Old Trafford was definitely building, and all the middle aged Billy Joel fans were politely queuing up for the toilet before buying cups of tea to take into the seating with them.

Consoling Sharon, who was by now consoling herself with a pouch of peanut M&M's and visibly furious with me for not buying a burger OUTSIDE the venue, I reassure her it's going to be a great gig and we should take our £210-worth of seats in the main arena. And so we walked out onto the terrace, and initially I thought "Yeah. Not bad". I knew it was going to be a side view. But then we were shown to our seat, almost at the furthest end of our row, and as we walked toward our £210-worth of seats, the view of the stage was rapidly diminishing. Going from "not bad". To "somewhat restricted view" to "restricted view" to "no fucking view at all". I re-checked my £210-worth of tickets. Yup. As I thought. No mention of Restricted View here.

Immediately around us, people were furious, waving their tickets in the air, looking for stewards to complain to. How could this be? We ALL thought we'd purchased *reasonably* good tickets for that money.

Security and stewards were less than useless. Minimum waged temporary staff not getting that a lot of people had paid a lot of money for a one off concert which is unlikely to be repeated for many years to come. They. Didn't. Want. To. Know.

I looked across at Sharon. She was sat in her seat, resigned to no view, just staring at her hands which were sticky with residual tomato ketchup. This was only our first night in Manchester and nothing was going as planned. The thought of spending all day Sunday walking around Manchester was too much to bear, and so I set about re-arranging train tickets to come home a night early and was prepared to forgo our second night at the Rembrandt. Obviously none of this was refundable. Obviously.

By now the stadium was full. I heard the cheer as Billy walked on stage. Heard it. Couldn't see it. Opening with *My Life*, then into *Pressure*, it was *sounding* great. This was followed by *The Entertainer*. Three fantastic opening songs in an order I've never heard before at a Billy Joel concert. But it was so frustrating. We couldn't even see the screens.

Billy was on entertaining form this evening. "I know what you're thinking," he said to the audience in his famous New York accent, "what the hell happened to that guy?". "Well. Let me tell you. From where I'm sitting, some of you don't look so great either."

"I'm 69 now," he said. "I used to like that number".

And then I caught my first glimpse of the man. He lent forward, looked back and up to the side seats where we were sat and said: "Whoa. They're the shitty seats. Hope you guys didn't pay much for them." Then he disappeared again. I could have screamed. "Only £210, Billy." I don't think he heard me. Or even actually gave that much of a shit.

And then we're off. Possibly the best concert I've never seen. Billy sounded great, and was clearly having a blast. Highlights for me were *Vienna, Half A Mile Away, Sometimes A Fantasy* and, of course, *Scenes From An Italian Restaurant*.

Billy used his only UK gig as a chance to indulge in some of his favourite British bands and there were covers from The Beatles, Rolling Stones, The Animals and even Queen. Once again, Mike DelGuidice brought the house down with his rendition of *Nessun Dorma*.

The concert ended with *We Didn't Start The Fire, Uptown Girl* (ugh), *It's*

Still Rock n Roll To Me and then *You Maybe Right.*

Two and a half hours of faultless music. Errr. *Listening* to a live band was, I guess, the next best thing to *seeing* them.

As we tried to walk out of the stadium at the same time as 70,000+ other people, hungry and disappointed overall, we reluctantly made our way over to the merchandise stand, situated not inside the stadium, but outside in a car park?

More out of loyalty than a sense of "I've just seen a great gig", I purchased the "retro" t-shirt (£45), baseball cap (£25) and badge set (£20). I was haemorrhaging cash at an alarming rate now but just felt because I couldn't actually *see* the concert, I needed to remind myself with this merchandise I was actually *there*. However, I will NEVER see (or listen to) another live concert at Old Trafford again. Never.

Leaving the venue was just as disorganised as walking there. Poor signage. No explanation of public transport and more unhelpful stewards. But then we got our break. Probably the luckiest moment of the weekend. We managed to jump in a cab and get back to the City ahead of all the crowds. I didn't realise it at the time, but this was the start of MY Billy Joel moment.

CHAPTER TWENTY TWO
FAMOUS LAST WORDS

I'd heard a whisper the band had checked into Manchester's most luxurious hotel, The Lowry.

Unsurprisingly, it was some distance away from the Rembrandt where I had splashed out £75 per night (not including breakfast). I'm guessing The Lowry was considerably more.

To make matters a little confusing, The Lowry Hotel is nowhere near The Lowry in Manchester. I couldn't get my head around this either.

The Lowry describes itself as a "spectacular waterside building housing theatres, galleries, restaurants and bars." I've been there. Spectacular isn't quite the word I would use. Anyway, initially, I thought The Lowry Hotel might be situated at The Lowry. It isn't. They're about five miles apart.

So. We're fighting through the crowds at Old Trafford trying to make our way back to the city from the venue. Thousands and thousands of us. This wasn't going to be easy.

I'd already made my mind up that we were going to go to The Lowry *Hotel* for post-concert drinks in the hope that some members of the band might make their way down to the bar to chill out.

Getting there wasn't going to be easy. I wasn't sure exactly where it was, despite looking on maps and ringing the hotel for directions.

We shuffled along with the crowd in the general direction of the main road with a view to catching a bus or tram to the city. Taxis were nowhere to be seen.

But then we stumbled on a taxi driver having a dispute with a group of four drunks. The driver clearly didn't want to risk people throwing up in his cab and he was refusing point blank to take them. At one point the loudest and most obnoxious of the group pulled out a fistful of cash: "I'll give you a hundred pounds" he slurred. "Just get us out of here," he said. Everyone was desperate to get out of the area.

With the drunk still leaning in his cab window, the driver drove off. He'd spotted us watching the scene and pulled up alongside us. "Cab?" he said, shouting through the passenger window. "Yes please I said," shoving Sharon in the back as quickly as possible.

"How much to The Lowry Hotel?" I asked. "£20" was the reply. I'd figured it couldn't be more than a five mile cab ride, but right now I was willing to pay anything. Well. I say anything. But not £100. The difference was, we weren't drunk and the driver was more than willing to take us.

And so we sped away from the area, way ahead of the majority of the crowd who had been catching us up like an unstoppable tidal wave. Down backstreets and alleyways, this driver knew the city and we made good progress leaving everyone behind.

We pulled up outside the 165 bedroom Lowry Hotel, a rather bland looking concrete and glass building which wasn't really shouting "luxury".

The hotel's website seems to disagree, saying: "Where things happen for the modern luxury generation. Stay at The Lowry Hotel and you're putting yourself at the centre of the action — a five-star contemporary hotel where Salford meets Manchester on the banks of the River Irwell. Here the dynamic spirit of England's north is reflected in our dynamic bar and restaurant, while you can count on our warm convivial service the moment you arrive. The result? A unique experience delivering luxury, vibrancy and a seductive measure of Northern fun."

"Things happen for the modern luxury generation"? Does that sentence actually mean anything? "Northern fun"?? We hadn't had much so far.

The website continues: "Located on the original site of the printing company where cult British comics, 'The Dandy' and 'The Beano', were created, Manchester's luxury Lowry Hotel has never lost its sense of fun. Since opening this iconic hotel in April 2001, there have been many Lowry antics. We won't tell you about them, not just because we're discreet about those who stay, but because The Lowry Hotel is less about history as it is about you and the city's present energy."

I wish I'd read this about the hotel before we got there. I could have brought a whole new meaning to "sense of fun" with the guarantee that the hotel wouldn't tell anyone about it. Result!

Anyway. My guess was that Billy would be staying in the Charles Forte Suite at the hotel. A penthouse so huge, it even has its own Baby Grand piano. Mmmm. That might come in handy for rehearsals?

But I digress. The taxi screeches to a halt outside the lobby and the concierge opens the cab door for us as smoke rises from the overheated tyres. This was approximately 20 minutes after the end of the show. We'd made good time.

Sharon, carrying a bag of valuable BJ merchandise, felt a little uncomfortable as we made our way upstairs to the bar which is strangely called The River Bar. Strange because it is on the first floor (that's second floor for my American readers), and so not by the river at all. "Act like you belong here" was my advice and reassurance to her. We both held our heads up high and walked past the bell boys.

Once upstairs, I spotted a table for two. I told Sharon to sit down and I would get us a drink at the bar. The lighting was very low and I was surprised how quiet it was, considering this is Manchester's top hotel.

I walked to the bar and spotted a familiar face. It was none other than Billy's long time saxophonist, Mark Rivera. "Hello Mark," I said and reached out a hand which he was happy to shake, before he stepped away from the bar. Result!

He looked a little confused, and I perhaps ought to point out that I was wearing a maroon coloured T Shirt emblazoned with the words "**NEW YORK CITY**" and a white New York Yankees baseball cap. So my English accent certainly didn't match my appearance and had clearly thrown him.

As he moved away, I leant on the bar drumming my fingers as I waited to be served. Just then, I became aware of an American accent at the bar. I glanced over to my right and, just a few feet away from me was a bloke in his late sixties, wearing a blue baseball cap and scarf sitting on a bar stool eating what looked like chicken nuggets out of a basket.

This guy looked *exactly* like Billy Joel. Hang on a minute. Surely not? I did a double take. He was chatting to a couple of older American guys who were clearly a part of his inner circle.

Fuck me! It's only Billy bloody Joel sat at the bar next to me. Eating chicken nuggets. My head went dizzy. I hopped from foot to foot and my mouth went dry. Since the age of 12 I had waited for this moment. I wanted to ask him all about Brenda and Eddie; Who was Leyna?; Everybody Loves *WHO* Now?; Was Laura really written about his mother? Why was he always so angry?

Now. Any Billy Joel fan can tell you that he has answered those questions a thousand times, and there was nothing original I could think of to say to him.

"Breathe. Compose yourself", I thought. I needed a plan. This was going to be my only opportunity. I know. I'll ask Sharon.

Risking losing the moment, I half walked/ran with arms rigid by my side so as to not to draw attention to myself (failed), stood behind her and put both hands on her shoulders and said in a whisper/shout through gritted teeth: "Billy's at the bar!"

Immediately she picked up the bags of merchandise and we both walked/ran arms rigid by our sides back to the bar.

Sensing this was my now or never moment, I leant in, hand outstretched. Remember, I'm dressed as a New Yorker here, so Billy possibly thought I was some long lost friend from his native Long Island who just happened to be staying at The Lowry (hotel), not a fan from the gig because there was no way I could have got back so quickly.

So. What do you think my opening line was?

I needed to try and be original, and so thought I'd use a quote from one of his own songs. So. Here it is:

"Man. What are YOU doing here?"

Billy looked completely bemused. And I have to say, not particularly happy.

As I shook his hand anyway I added: "That was a great concert. Really enjoyed it. Thanks for all your music. By the way, this is my wife Sharon."

I looked over my shoulder and Sharon raised a hand and, for some unknown reason, in a really high pitched voice could only say "Hi".

Billy said: "Thank you".

I got the impression he wasn't in the mood for selfies, autographs, sharing a pint or even a chicken nugget with me. Or actually even smiling.

And although this would likely be the only time in either of our lives that we would spend any quality time together (not sure Billy was too concerned about this), I felt it was not the best time to raise the issue about the "shitty" concert seats we had just sat in for two and a half hours.

I didn't want to linger like some weird demented fan (a-hem), so I thought it best to leave things on good terms where they were and say our goodbyes.

Sharon and I went back to our seats.

I felt weird. Happily disappointed, if that's even possible. Over the years I'd spent untold thousands of pounds in Britain and America going to concerts, finding out about Billy's youth and reliving some of his childhood experiences in Hicksville and Long Island. Even having dinner in a certain Italian Restaurant.

Now I'd met my hero. A man whose words and music did so much to shape my own life as an angst riddled teenager. It's like I'd found the final piece of the puzzle that had been eluding me all my life, but it wasn't a perfect fit.

The bar was filling up rapidly as other concert-goers started to arrive. Finally an atmosphere was building. The hushed conversations when we had arrived in the bar were being replaced by chatter and laughter.

But I sat alone with my thoughts. Thoughts of that teenager sitting in his sister's bedroom listening to *The Stranger* for the first time, enjoying the story telling of *Scenes From An Italian Restaurant*.

Crowds were building, and Billy, looking uncomfortable with the large group that were now starting to gather around him, decided it was time to make an exit. I watched him as he walked to the elevator.

Sharon interrupted my thoughts: "Are you okay?" she asked. "Yeah", I said. "Bit weird".

I was euphoric about meeting my idol. But disappointed I had no photographic evidence. Or an autograph. In this Facebook world we live in, if there's no video or photo, it didn't happen.

"Listen," said Sharon. "I know you met him. I was there when you leant in and shook his hand."

We had been lucky to catch that cab and get to the bar when we did. No other fans had met Billy that night. Just me and Sharon.

I ordered another drink. Just then Tommy Byrnes – Billy's lead guitarist – walked past.

"Hey Tommy. Great show man," I said. He stopped in his tracks. "Thanks man. Really appreciate it."

I shook his hand. A real genuine guy, happy to chat to a complete stranger but someone who appreciates his talent.

"Tommy," I said. "Last time we saw you you were playing guitar with Mike DelGuidice and Big Shot in Rocky Point".

Now, those of you who had been paying attention in this book will remember that it was at Dek's restaurant in Rocky Point that Dek told us of his dislike of all things Billy Joel.

"They hate us in Rocky Point," laughed Tommy. "We play outdoors. Roads get closed and all the restaurants moan they lose business 'cos of us!"

Tommy happily posed for a selfie before taking time to chat to other fans who had made it to The Lowry (hotel).

The time was getting on for 2am. Sharon was knackered. Time for a taxi home.

So. As the taxi drove us passed the urinating women in the streets, and the drunks fighting outside the clubs on our way back to the Rembrandt hotel, I could sense our time in Manchester would soon be coming to an end. Thank God.

It was 4.30am when we got back to the hotel. A transvestite was throwing up not far from the entrance. Club Tropicana underneath our bedroom was packed and in full swing. I can remember they were playing Dead Or Alive's *You Spin Me Round (Like A Record)*, followed by *Come on Eileen* by Dexy's Midnight Runners. There wasn't going to be much sleep tonight.

And so the next morning, having booked yet more train tickets, we were homeward bound to Milton Keynes.

As I read on-line reviews of last night's gig, a BBC news article popped up on my phone:

"Furious Billy Joel Fans Demand Refund" was the headline.

Turns out the riggers had built the stage in the wrong place on the pitch at Old Trafford. The stage had been built too far forward rendering thousands of side view seats useless. Brilliant.

CHAPTER TWENTY THREE

THE ULTIMATE STORY

No-one has a better Billy Joel story to tell than multi-talented musician Mike DelGuidice. No-one.

It's the ultimate twist of a fan who doesn't just get to meet his idol, but gets to be a part of the act.

There are many Billy Joel tribute bands out there, particularly on Long Island, but no-one could have predicted what was to happen one special night when Mike's band, called Big Shot, were joined on stage by a very special guest....Billy Joel himself.

Imagine that. Billy Joel getting up on stage to perform Billy Joel songs with a Billy Joel tribute band. It just blows your mind.

I was excited to hear this story from the man himself. I wanted to listen intently as Mike DelGuidice talked excitedly about the moment he met his idol for the first time.

Only problem was, I could hardly hear him at all.

You see, when Michael graciously agreed to be interviewed by me for this book, I thought it would be cool to talk to him prior to a sound check for Big Shot at The Iridium club in New York City. Big mistake.

Ordinarily things would have worked out fine. The Iridium were cool with hosting the interview, and had a table and chairs set aside for us. But there were a couple of things no-one could have prepared for:

Due to traffic and transport delays, Mike was an hour late, which meant other members of the band were already there setting up and tuning instruments, and;

Mike had almost completely lost his voice due to laryngitis, and was quite rightly trying to hold on to what little voice he had left for the show.

And so the combination of the band tuning up, and Mike having little voice, meant that the machine I was using to record the interview was barely registering his voice.

And I suspect you, dear readers, were thinking that interviewing rock stars was easy. Glamorous even. But it's stressful. Very stressful. Let me tell you.

But this isn't about me. It's about Mike. And ultimately Billy. So. Get over it. Anyway. Back to the story…

Big Shot is no ordinary tribute band. In addition to Mike, other band members include guitarist Tommy Byrnes and drummer Chuck Burgi both of whom are current members of Billy Joel's band. And the rest of the band is made up of some of New York's finest musicians, including Carmine Giglio on keyboards, Nick Dimichino on bass and saxophonist John Scarpulla.

And when they're tuning up, they make a lot of noise. Especially when you're sat just feet away.

But as we settled down for the interview, I was able to hear how Mike beat all the odds to overcame a congenital kidney condition which threatened his life and required several surgeries; how he once donned a wig and dark glasses as part of his Billy Joel Tribute Act ("I did it once. Never again"), and how he describes the almost heavenly harmonies he is able to achieve when singing with his hero Billy Joel.

Growing up in Miller Place, Long Island, Michael's early taste in music was heavily influenced by his father and his brother.

"There are lots of gigs and tons of talent that comes out of Long Island. It oozes out of the place and so I was fortunate enough to grow up there.

"The music thing started pretty early for me in terms of musical influences. My father's choice was pretty diverse, he loved everything including Billy and Elton John. My brother John was into heavy rock," said Mike.

And so at the tender age of just 14, Mike scored his first gig at a place called Pipers Pit which led onto a regular gig at a piano bar.

I ask Mike about his childhood, and that congenital condition. Something he has never talked about on the record before. He sighs and looks to the sky, appearing unwilling to talk about painful memories.

After a pause, he says: "Most of the real severe stuff happened before I was able to perform, and it has left its marks everywhere.

"I had tons of surgeries and as a kid it really affected me going out. I've got scars on my back, but the scars become a part of you. Thank God that I survived," he says.

The conversation quickly turns back to the music, and Mike is keen to talk about the Billy Joel song that was an early influence: "*Scenes From An Italian Restaurant* is probably the song that got me hooked, but it was watching Billy's live performance of that song on Live From Long Island that did it.

"I always heard his stuff on the radio and I liked his songs, but when I saw him in concert in that video, that was when I was first, like 'Wow'.

"*Scenes* was an album cut, it wasn't a hit, and so anything I'd heard on the radio up to that point wasn't that song, but when I heard it live, it was like 'Holy crap'.

"It was the story telling. He just creates this stuff by just being himself and because he's famous, everything he says becomes nostalgic and you can relate to anything".

Did a teenage Mike find his musical taste at an early age was at odds with his peers who would have, perhaps, been into more contemporary music at that time?

"I guess that all depended on the crowd you hung out with," said Mike. "Nobody on Long Island would diss Billy Joel. You'll never hear anybody say anything bad. They might say 'I don't dig his music, I'm a rock guy or a metal guy', but nobody's ever gonna say that he's not ridiculously talented or one of the greatest song writers ever."

But growing up on Long Island, Mike acknowledges he didn't have many options: "It was music or bust for me," he says. "I could have followed my family's long history of landscaping and done that, which is noble and hard work, but it wasn't for me, you know. I just knew it was gonna be music.

"I was at High School cutting class and I was playing *Honesty*, and someone said to me 'You sound like him a lot', and that started the piano bar thing.

"*Honesty* is a hard one to sing. It's not easy. But then I realised his popularity, and not only that, but I was pretty natural at playing his stuff, and I got a pretty good following, and so it made sense."

It was at about this time that Mike had the first idea to set up Big Shot: "I didn't know tribute bands existed. But I was like, how can anyone sing just one artist the whole night? It was unheard of then.

"Every band I was in was Top 40. Nobody was doing one artist the whole night. But in Vegas though, it was a regular thing. To me it was cheese and I didn't want to be in a cheese like band.

"All I know is this, I'm not wearing a wig or anything. We were going to do that at the beginning to make it more like a show, and I think I put a wig on once and I was like 'Nah. That's that'.

"I've always tried so hard not to become in anyway a lookalike act. I hate the word tribute. It's become demeaning."

And so, just relying on his talent and the music to make a success of Big Shot, word started to spread: "Yeah, it surprised me. I know that Billy's music is going to work in a bar, I know that. Put a crowd there and his music alone could probably sustain the night, and that's how popular his music is.

"So if you're in a fun kind of mood, it doesn't matter who you are, you are going to have a great night listening to his music. It's a testimony to his music more than anything."

But it was in 2010 that things switched up a gear. Billy took time out of touring to have both hips replaced. Tommy spotted an opportunity and contacted members of Billy's band.

"I was making a couple of changes to the band. The guys were getting bored and it just wasn't feeling good.

"I knew Tommy (Byrnes) from a long time ago – we'd played together and we had jammed a couple of times. This was back in the days of the *Movin' Out* show, so we met that way. I was looking for a new guitarist and Tommy said yes, because that's him. He's a worker."

Mike managed to persuade Billy's drummer Chuck Burgi to get on board, and so the new, supercharged Big Shot was formed.

Rapidly outgrowing the smaller venues, it wasn't long before Big Shot were selling out theatres, filling the void left by Billy Joel himself as he recovered from hip replacement surgery.

As 2013 loomed, Billy was getting ready to get back on the road again, and so word went out to his band that it was time to get rehearsing. And this is when things started to get interesting for Mike.

While members of Billy's touring band met up to rehearse, Billy wouldn't necessarily show, so Tommy asked Mike to "stand in" at rehearsals and "be Billy".

"I felt like I was there to fill the void, and at the end of the day they just needed someone to fill in. It was Tommy again. He said would I be Billy's stunt double. There wasn't much thinking needed to take that part!"

And then one day, Billy himself showed up at a rehearsal, and he was impressed with what he was listening to. As rehearsals progressed, Mike and Billy would regularly sing together.

Mike explains: "Where he had doubled himself on the albums, he wanted a vocal double and I was doing a lot of that with him, and it was record quality.

"Our voices together are really very interesting. I sound like a younger Billy, and he has a very baritone tone now, and so I guess his tone and my tone together creates this unbelievable illusion and it's just incredible.

"I hear his voice in my right ear, and my voice in my left, and the result is like 'Oh my God'. It's bizarre and it's incredible. Now I find myself watching his vocal and holding out my notes the same way so that it is tight. It's a lot to think about."

Impressed with how things were going, Mike was asked to join Billy on the European leg of his upcoming tour. Initially Mike thought it was to sit in for sound checks, but once there, he realised he was to be part of the band.

"The hardest thing about getting in the band was taking over other people's roles. Was I going to be around? Was I a flash in the pan? I didn't know what they were thinking.

"I figured it was probably just a temporary thing, and at the end of the London gig, I asked Brian Ruggles (Billy's long-term sound man), if I was sticking around or what the hell was going on. I'd almost played the entire tour now.

"We were at the Apollo in London, and I followed Brian downstairs and Billy told me then. That was the night I actually officially found out I was in the band."

Some members of the band have been with Billy for more than 30 years. How does Mike feel he fits in?: "It's awesome. I feel very easy in Billy's company. He's very relaxed. But if someone plays the opening chords to Just The Way You Are wrong, he can't stand it. But that's because he cares."

If ever Mike needed reassurance that he was now well established and part of Billy's inner circle, that came one night during a Big Shot gig at the Paramount Theatre in Huntington, Long Island. Midway through a gig in 2016, Billy showed up and joined Michael on stage: "I'd waited 17 years for that moment, hoping it would happen," said Mike.

"If you watch the video on YouTube you can see how I feel. I'd been playing with HIS band, and then five years later he comes to see MY show. It was weird. He was sat at the piano and I didn't know what to do. I was like 'Do you want me to go outside?' and he was like 'It's your show!'"

And this seemed to be a good time to bring the interview to an end. Mike was clearly unwell, struggling to speak and knowing that he had a full show of Billy's rarities to play ahead of him.

After posing for a couple of photographs with me, Mike joined the rest of the band on stage, while Sharon and I sat back and watched the sound check, secretly wondering if Billy was going to walk in and help the guys continue to set up.

The Iridium is an intimate basement venue a short walk from Time Square, and the perfect venue to enjoy a show like this. Several "Billys" were lined up to help Mike out, including David Clark and Wade Preston. It's quite clear there is a close bond between Billy tribute singers.

The show didn't disappoint. Rare Billy Joel tracks performed brilliantly, up close and personal and demonstrating that even if you only know Billy's hits, you will be equally impressed by these lesser known numbers.

There's nothing precious about Mike DelGuidice and the other members of Big Shot. They're a down to earth bunch equally at home playing to 50,000 or 150. They give it their all, and at the end of the show, it's photo's all round.

*Following on from this interview, Mike cancelled a number of upcoming Big Shot shows due to severe and worsening laryngitis. Fortunately he has now made a full recovery and is back on the road.

> *"My wedding song is You're My Home and we ended the night, as we end all celebratory nights with arms around one another swaying back and forth to Piano Man."* **Doug Cotler, location not stated.**

CHAPTER TWENTY FOUR
NEW YORK STATE OF MIND

And so our 2018 trip to America was coming to an end.

We had achieved so much in terms of research, fun and making new friends. And so by way of a final farewell, we headed back to Oyster Bay for one last lunch.

This was to be our third visit to Oyster Bay on this trip. Our taxi driver friend John Marchut had insisted we visit the Oyster Fest 2018 which had been held a few days earlier. The Festival is a family orientated weekend that attracts thousands of people to the village.

And John was our closest thing to family on Long Island, so it seemed fitting that we go with him. We picked him up from his Hicksville taxi rank and he had expertly planned the day for us. He advised us to make use of the park and ride facility just outside Oyster Bay, and once there, he proudly guided us through the incredible food court and craft fair, pausing briefly at the petting zoo, before watching the, er, pirate show. That evening we sat outdoors drinking beer together while enjoying a Billy Joel/Elton John tribute band, which was a little surreal.

Anyway, back to our last day and last visit to Oyster Bay. The sun was shining as we drove along the tree lined route into town, the homes and houses becoming larger and neater the closer we got.

There was an element of sadness that this trip was coming to an end. Sharon and I chatted excitedly as we drove into town, both of us reflecting on this memorable trip.

We talked about how we got to know the real Long Island with John as our guide, and chatted about Yvonne who had been our AirBnB host in Hicksville.

We laughed as we recalled paying a further visit to Debbie-Lou in Sag Harbor before having a drink at the American Legion Club next door to Billy's Sag Harbor home.

And then of course there were the rock stars we had met; The irrepressible Larry Russell who talked about his love/hate/love affair with Billy Joel, exclusively opening his heart to us in a way that no-one else could.

The time spent straining our ears listening to Michael DelGuidice telling us his story of super-fan turned Billy Joel band member. And then the same evening making a new friend in ultra-cool guitarist Tommy Byrnes who would rather make apple sauce than throw a TV out of a hotel room, before watching them both perform a Big Shot show in New York City. These were fun times.

At the Big Shot gig we met Jack Scala, who says he is the real-life inspiration for the song about drug dealer Captain Jack. The full story is way too controversial to reproduce here. Was he the drug dealer Billy was referring to? Hassles guitarist Richard McKenna has confirmed it: "He was a Hassles follower who kept us happy, if you know what I mean," Richard told me.

We had been invited onto Govs Radio in Hicksville by Tony Walker and Sallie O'Neill to talk about the book and ended up staying on air for almost two hours, together with host Eric Skjeveland. Eric reminded me of the actor Jack Black –but more outrageous! In fact, Tony and Eric purchased the first two copies of the book, paying $20 each. Cash. Thanks guys.

Somehow, in-between all this, we walked and walked around New York City, taking in the sights and the shops; became experts travelling on the Subway and knew the Long Island Railroad timetable off by heart. We made a point of visiting Trump Tower and riding the gold escalator made infamous by the current President of the United States, before stopping off at the NBC store to buy a Seinfeld t-shirt. And then having lunch at Tom's Restaurant – the exterior made famous by America's favourite sitcom.

We even took time to drive to New Jersey. It turned out to be an expensive trip due to being in a hire car and not in a position to pay all the tolls as we went. Thanks Dollar for the $171 admin bill you sent us for taking care of that.

We visited Asbury Park to pay homage to, of course, Bruce Springsteen, and we loved the rocky, hippy vibe of the town as we strolled along its famous boardwalk, taking in the derelict buildings and chic bars and restaurants.

We explored the Jersey Shore as we drove to Atlantic City, an unfriendly and grubby mini Vegas (which did boast an exceptional outdoor designer outlet mall). But a place I won't be returning to anytime soon.

Was this trip a vacation, or a fact finding mission? It was, of course, both. I had spent a fortune, but I didn't mind contributing to the American tourist economy. Just a shame the exchange rate was against me.

Poor Sharon was exhausted, but I was still on a high. I could easily have spent another week or so hanging with my American buddies, living a Friends/Seinfeld life-style. I was most definitely in a New York State of Mind and I didn't want to leave.

CHAPTER TWENTY FIVE

SOUVENIR

It was 1pm on a Tuesday as we drove into Oyster Bay – our final day of this eventful October 2018 visit.

We had to be back on the road by 4pm if we were to make our American Airlines flight from JFK to London.

Once in town, we found ourselves parking just a short distance away from 20th Century Cycles, Billy's motorbike showroom, which is usually only open to the public at the weekends.

As we walked past the showroom, the roller shutter was up, so we were able to have another look around at all the amazing bikes which are either from an era long ago, or transformed to look like motorbikes from an era long ago. Billy's long term mechanic Scott was happy to talk to us about the collection which he is clearly very proud of.

Scott was interested to hear our London accents and correctly guessed we were British. "Do you know the British Billy Joel? I think his name is Elio?," he asked.

We explained we were good friends with Elio. "Yeah. He showed up with a group of people when we were closed one day, so we let them in and showed them around and he dropped off a bunch of DVDs and CDs for Billy. He's pretty talented. He even looks a little like Billy," said Scott.

We headed off up Audrey Avenue, pausing in the October sunshine to look in the shop windows as we strolled hand in hand.

We made our way to Taby's, the diner where 10 days earlier we lunched with our new friend John Marchut. We got a table near the street. In our old familiar place. We chuckled as we tried to imagine Billy walking through the door the day after his most recent wedding to collect his take out lunch.

I took a moment to look around this charming but fading diner, which probably hasn't been redecorated since the 1970s. Its dark wood tables and slightly smoky windows creating a unique atmosphere. Combined with the smell of burgers and French Fries I was transported back to a time when "salad" was a dirty word.

We ordered the deluxe burger to share and sat quietly as we both gazed out of the window and along the Main Street of a town made famous by Billy The Kid.

Conscious of the time and our impending flight, we settled the cheque and had a final look round as we stood up to leave. It was 3pm.

The autumn (fall) sun was still shining as we strolled back along Audrey Avenue and past number 34, which is the home to Billy's company, Maritime Music Inc.

As we turned the corner by 20th Century Cycles I noticed an incredible baby blue Harley Davidson parked in the street outside. We crossed the road and walked toward it. As we passed the showroom, the roller shutter was down now, but we both looked in and both recognised a familiar figure talking to Scott.

Wearing a black leather jacket, jeans and brown baseball cap was the creator of the songs of my youth. The musical genius who has sold 200 million albums around the world, broken concert attendance records at the chapel of Madison Square Garden and was a miserable bastard when I saw him at The Lowry Hotel in Manchester.

Sharon flipped out: "HE'S IN THERE!"

I knew that keeping cool was important. Particularly as he was just about to walk through the door right in front of me.

And there I was. Face to face with Billy The Kid in a town known as Oyster Bay, Long Island. Like a scene from a Spaghetti Western, our eyes locked and for a moment I thought I was going to get the steely-eyed stare Billy is famous for if he doesn't want to talk. I'd seen that face in Manchester four months earlier.

Just as I leaned forward to politely ask for a photograph, fearful of the response, I was elbowed out the way by Sharon who, in a strange high pitched voice, said: "Hello Billy. We're from England!".

"She's blown it," I thought. I was just about to turn away in shame when Billy broke into a huge smile and bellowed "YOU DON'T SAY?!" in his cheeky Long Island/New York accent.

"Do you mind if we have a photograph together?" I asked, uncertain of his reply. He looked at me, then at Sharon, shrugged his shoulders and said "Sure. Why not?".

And there we were. Taking photos; Me and Billy; Sharon and Billy; Me and Billy again; Billy on his own; Billy with his bike. Did I mention me and Billy? Laughing. Joking. Talking. Smiling. For ten minutes.

As part of my "Just in case we bump into Billy" kit, Sharon had a pen and piece paper and moved in for the ultimate Billy memento. "Can we get your autograph?" asked Sharon, as I filmed on my mobile phone.

Smiling the whole time he boomed: "Whad else do ya want? You want me to come round your house next or something?" This was great.

And so as Sharon handed him the pen and paper, Billy handed Sharon his motorbike helmet. Sharon turned to the camera and with a smile like I'd never seen before, she declared: "I'M HOLDING BILLY'S HELMET!" Now there's a sentence I never thought I'd hear.

And so I videoed the autograph moment, which proves it's genuine. As he handed the prized signature to me, he turned and said: "That'll be $8.50 please," still laughing and joking with us. We carried on talking about his beloved motorbikes. "It's reverse restoration," explained Billy. "We take new bikes and make them look old".

I told Billy we had the "shitty seats" at the Manchester gig. Shaking his head he said: "Man we had a lot of complaints about that. It was terrible." No apology or refund then? Didn't matter right now.

"Well, we're coming to see you at Wembley in June," I said. "Well. I probably won't see you!" was his good natured reply.

By now Billy had his helmet back, after prizing it from Sharon's grip, and he was preparing to head off. Billy is a famous biker. He has all the gear and looks every inch the part. Except, that was, up until the point I noticed his footwear.

You'd expect a $400 pair of Harley boots to match the bike, right? Or "engineer boots" as mentioned in the song. No! Billy was wearing a pair of comfy, fluffy black Ugg Boots! Probably just as expensive, but they didn't exactly scream Hells Angels.

After saying goodbyes, and with some difficulty – Billy's had a double hip replacement – he mounted his Harley, gave us a wave and headed off down the street, the roar of the Harley exhausts ringing in our ears.

"We've done it," said Sharon. "We've met Billy. Got the photos; got the autographs and had a chat. It's done," she said.

"Not quite," I thought. I still don't have that proper interview for this book. Have I just blown the only opportunity I may ever get?

I wasn't sure. But at the time of writing this, I don't think so. You see, I didn't feel the moment was quite right. Sure, I could have blurted out "Hey Billy. I'm writing a book about YOU". And he probably would have thought "Jerk". Or even worse, "No you're not. Get my lawyer on the phone."

But this was the best kind of brief encounter a fan could wish for. And a world away from the Billy Joel I had met a few months earlier in Manchester. Of course there were loads of questions I would have loved to ask, but I can save those for another day.

I was happy to laugh and joke in person with an American icon. Pass the time of day with the genius who had written *Just The Way You Are*. The legend who had lost millions, and then made millions by touring the world over and over and over again.

Love him or hate him, only a fool would doubt his talent. Or deny him his place in American cultural history. And Sharon and I were hanging out with him.

I'm hoping you're reading this Billy, so we can set something up properly. At your place. By the piano. It'll be a laugh, and like no other interview you've ever done before.

It was 4pm. Time for us to leave and head back to JFK. We'd met Billy Joel on the last hour of the last day of our trip. Cool or what?

CHAPTER TWENTY SIX
EPILOGUE

This book could have turned out quite differently. In fact, it might not have been about Billy Joel at all.

You see, soon after the release of The Stranger, another singer/songwriter from Brooklyn, New York was making a name for himself and winning the hearts of young girls all over Britain.

My sister owned many LP records at the time, not just The Stranger. And while that was her album of choice, the music of a certain Barry Manilow was also being played.

And as that young, impressionable 12 year old, as much as I loved the story of Brenda and Eddie, I was also enthralled by the story of Tony and Lola.

For those of you who haven't twigged yet, Lola was a showgirl with yellow feathers in her hair, and a dress cut down to there. Oh you know who I mean.

The venue was the *Copacabana* – apparently a hotspot just north of Havana. The fictional barman was called Tony, and they fell in love. You know the story. One night during a show, a mobster known as Rico attends the cabaret and tries his luck with Lola, but goes a little too far.

Standing up for his woman, Tony and Rico end up brawling until the club falls silent with a single gunshot.

Now, this was a musical story that also conjured up images in the same way as I had pictured Brenda and Eddie.

Not quite the seven minute plus masterpiece of *Scenes From An Italian Restaurant*, but a dramatic story nevertheless, and one that appealed to my youthful imagination.

As the song continues, we fast forward 30 years and the venue is no longer the glamourous nightspot it once was, it's now a disco and we're presented with an image of an ageing, alcoholic Lola, still wearing her show dress, like a demented bride, jilted at the altar.

But as much as I loved the song, and the dramatic story it told, I couldn't identify with "Tony" in the same way I thought I could identify with "Eddie".

Eddie had an edge to him. His leather jacket and tight blue jeans seemed to me a better image than some guy working behind a bar at a club. And I could have fallen in love with Brenda, but the image of a drunk, ageing Lola put me off.

And while the Copacabana Hotel which inspired the song (written by Manilow, Jack Feldman and Bruce Sussman) exists in Rio de Janerio, I've never felt the desire to visit the location and pay homage in the same way I wanted to see the Village Green and relive the excitement of hanging out with Brenda and Eddie.

This book writing process has made me examine the songs of my youth. It has been a fascinating trip down memory lane, examining why certain songs have had such a profound influence, and to really look at Billy Joel's catalogue and understand why his music stands out.

There have been other great songs along the way which have captured my imagination. The very first being The Beatles' *She's Leaving Home* from the Sgt Pepper album.

And then the others, in no particular order: Simon and Garfunkel's *America*; Neil Diamond's *Brooklyn Roads*; Neil Sedaka's *Queen Of 1964*; Rod Stewart's *Maggie May*; 10cc's *I'm Mandy, Fly Me* and Queen's *Bohemian Rhapsody*.

All of these songs tell brilliant stories. I know you'll know all of them, but when was the last time you listened to them. And I mean REALLY listened to them – with your eyes closed, picturing the story in your mind's eye as the music plays out?

But for me, only Billy Joel could consistently write provocative songs with a meaning, an edge, an ANGER that no other songwriter has conveyed throughout their entire songbook.

Listen to the lyrics of *Stiletto, Everybody Loves You Now*, She's *Always A Woman, Summer, Highland Falls*. All brilliant. I'd love to quote my favourite lines from each song, but the publishing rights to reproduce the lyrics here are way too expensive. So it's cheaper for you all to go out and buy the CDs (as if you didn't have them already!). That way I save a few bucks, and Billy makes a few (more) bucks. Everyone's happy.

I could go on and on and on with example after example of the brilliance of Billy's song writing. How it connects, but disconnects, how it loves, and then how it hates. But you have to listen for yourself. And if you don't "get it", then you've just wasted $14.99 reading this book.

But this is why I love Billy Joel. He might be grumpy, but he's a genius. And I just want to tell him that.

May, 2019.

ACKNOWLEDGEMENTS:

Elio Pace. Firstly, I must acknowledge the support and say a massive thank you to Elio who, not only was the first contributor to this project, but opened many doors for me on the other side of the Atlantic and acknowledged that I "get it" when it comes to loving the music of a certain Mr Billy Joel. Also big thanks to Handel Pianos Ltd (handelpianos.co.uk) of Sunningdale, Berkshire, UK for hosting the interview with Elio.

Larry Russell. Boy can this man talk! His vivid memories of those early days on the road were fascinating to listen to. I feel we have a friend in Larry, and Sharon and I will never forget the hours spent in his favourite booth at his favourite Upper West side diner. We love ya Larro!

Mike DelGuidice. I must admit to having a few sleepless nights in the run-up to our meeting with the Mighty Mike as communication lines between us were not the greatest. But on the evening of our interview, despite what turned out to be pretty serious laryngitis, he put on a brave face and literally talked until he lost his voice….an hour before putting on a remarkable show in New York City.

Mike Stutz. Billy Joel Facebook supremo Mike kept his cool while I was losing mine in New York and was happy – and gracious enough - to act as the communication conduit between myself and Mr DelGuidice, in addition to agreeing to be a part of this book himself. Respect, Mike and look forward to meeting you one day!

Tommy Byrnes. If I could have a rock star friend, I'd want it to be Tommy Byrnes. He's just so cool. He called me "Brother". We don't call each other "brother" in England, so I guess that means we're officially having a "Bromance". Again, we talked for hours and Tommy even agreed to meet up with me at Wembley Stadium. Rock n Roll, baby!

Michael Cavanaugh. The face – and the voice - of *Movin' Out*. Michael seemed to make this production his own and I loved listening to his story from Las Vegas piano bar to Broadway sensation. I also appreciate his willingness to be a part of this project.

John Marchut. Taxi driver extraordinaire and another new friend for Sharon and I in Hicksville. Who would have thought when we got in his cab at Hicksville Railroad Station two years ago, that, by chance, he would be the creator and operator of the most popular Billy Joel fan website on the internet: mylifebillyjoel.com. We loved our time with John as we toured Billy's childhood hangouts and homes and listened to his stories and his take on life. John is our Long Island family.

Richard McKenna. This man knew Billy Joel before Billy Joel knew Billy Joel! Guitarist Richard was there at the very beginning of a very special journey with The Hassles, and I feel honoured to have interviewed him for this book. His contribution adds an authenticity that seems to have been over-looked by other books chronicling the rise of an American Superstar. Thank you Richard. Keep on playing and I wish you well.

Rhys Clark. Billy's original drummer. Softly-spoken Rhys recalls memories of his early days with Billy not only as a musician, but as a friend. He acknowledges his contribution to the rise and rise of a global superstar with a sense of pride, and not an ounce of jealousy. I feel I just touched the surface of the stories Rhys and his wife Marilyn could tell about their time with Billy and his first wife Elizabeth. Perhaps for the revised edition of this book, Sharon and I can fly to LA for dinner. I feel we would get on just fine.

Liberty DeVitto. Perhaps the most reluctant contributor, but a contributor none the less. This book would be incomplete without something from the Hired Gun.

ACKNOWLEDGEMENTS:

David Clark. We met David for lunch in New York City. Not only is he "Billy" for the Lords of 52nd Street, but also for his own tribute show AND the Sigma reunion! I suggested he and Elio Pace get together for a duelling pianos show. Now that's a gig I'd like to see.

Tony Walker, Sallie O'Neill and shock jock **Eric Skjeveland**. Sharon and I spent a memorable two hours talking about this book on their show at Govs Radio in Hicksville, AND Tony and Eric officially bought the first two copies – even before I'd finished writing it. Now there's faith!

Debbie Lou Houdek. The world needs more people like Debbie Lou. Funny, eccentric and our Sag Harbor "insider". Thanks for all the Billy tips and pointers and helping us like you did. If ever you visit Sag Harbor, be sure to visit her store, Blooming Shells.

Kevin Mocker. World class photographer AND a Billy Joel fan! Thanks for your support, Kevin, and the photographs which are credited elsewhere in the book.

Jan Henderson. Forever my Editor. Thanks for agreing to profe reed, make corections and suggesttions. Invaluible.

Billy Joel's Inner Circle. This book was written entirely without help, guidance or contributions from Billy's team. Totally unauthorised. Yeah baby!

Billy Joel. Looking forward to being a passenger in your side car as you give me the Billy The Kid Tour of Oyster Bay, before meeting up with our wives for lunch at Taby's. My treat.

LISTEN TO WHAT THE FANS SAID

"I met all the band at the hotel before his Manchester gig. I'd heard Billy would be meeting his agent in the bar after the gig, so I raced back and saw him sitting at the bar. As I got near him his tour manager blocked me so I politely asked if I could say a quick hello, but was told NO. I waited for him to walk to the lifts and asked if he would sign something for me. I asked him to sign my arm but he said "It'll wash off". I told him I was going to get it tattooed. He signed my arm very slowly and carefully. I shook his hand and thanked him. Meeting Billy was a dream come true. And yes, I did get that autograph tattooed!" **Tina Canderton, London, UK.**

"I saw Billy Joel twice in '76 at Penn State University in REC Hall. The first time the audio blew up and he returned just six months later. The concert at the Academy of Music in Philadelphia was remarkable. He was about to appear at Carnegie Hall and he seemed so excited in the spring of '77." **Errol Kofsky, location not given.**

"The first time I heard Billy Joel was from a Disney movie called Oliver & Company and I saw it on Disney Channel back in 2008 when I was in Vineland, NJ and the song I heard was called Why Should I Worry. Ever since I saw that movie and heard that song I've been a fan of Billy Joel. He's been my idol and inspiration for the longest time and I went to see him at the BB&T Center at Sunrise, Florida, on Saturday January 11th, 2014 at 8pm. It was the best concert of a lifetime. If there's a biopic movie about him then I would absolutely love to play him. He'll always have a special place in my heart." **Samuel Echevarria Jr, Fl**

"I was a fan of Billy's since before I was born! My parents were fans and would often play his music. I grew up listening to Billy. I remember seeing Billy for the first time in concert and crying when he first began singing! It

was so surreal to see him in person after constantly listening to his music at home. I'm 46 now and my love for Billy and his music has not really changed over the years... if anything it has gotten stronger! Billy's music calms me, inspires me and picks me up when I'm sad. Billy Joel is a legend, an amazing talent and I will always be a fan of his. Always." **Melanie Yormark Brooklyn, NY**.

"I hope 2019 is a best seller for you." **Cjack Scala**

"Graduated Berner HS 1974, LIU CWPost 1978. Saw his concert at Post in 77, also multiple times at My Fathers Place and Atlanta. Just retired after teaching choral music 40 years as Choral Director Walhalla HS, Walhalla SC. Developed a Presentation Skills course and curriculum for High School students based on Billy's An Evening of Questions and Answers and maybe a little music with Billy Joel. Presented this curriculum at many educational conferences. Billy has been my musical mentor and age / life skills example for many years. At my last (retirement) concert, I led the audience of parents and guests in a singalong of Piano Man with me on the keys. For many years, I've been referred to as "The Billy Joel of Walhalla SC"." **John Fallon Originally from Massapequa NY**.

"Got hooked on Piano Man (the song) in college and I thought I gotta see him in concert. Just as someone predicted I knew easily more than half of the songs and was able to get out just in time to make the train home, back in 2005 or so. I remember sending my tour program in to get autographed and got it returned to me autographed just in time for Christmas. I was so stoked. Been a huge fan ever since." **Jason 'jayman' Porta, Originally from Altoona, PA**.

"I had the pleasure of meeting Billy in a bar in Glasgow in May 1994. He was playing a concert the next night. I asked him what Scottish tune he planned on playing as the intro to My Life. I suggested Scotland the Brave and Billy said okay. I told friends the next day that I'd met Billy and of our conversation and they didn't believe me. But sure enough Billy mentioned his visit to the Horseshoe Bar at the gig and duly played Scotland the Brave before launching into My Life. In the bar Billy also signed a newspaper I had bought earlier that day that had a picture and article about his upcoming Glasgow concert. I still have the newspaper." **Scott Reid, location not stated.**

"I was 14 years old when I heard Scenes for the first time. It just lit me up inside. So much that when I was 16 and an usher at a local theatre where Johnny Mathis was playing, I heard some "older patrons" mention how they felt sorry for my generation because we don't have any performers that will still be around when we grew up. I stepped in and asked if they ever heard of Billy Joel. They said no. I told them to notice his music because I guarantee he will be singing when I am your age....I am 56." **Kathleen Luken, Hobart, IN**

"So my dad left my mom in 1979... I was nine...he put a cassette tape with a recording of My Life on her dresser and walked out... he was very proud of that gesture and yet I still love that song." **Shira Rachel Lipton-Yacker, location not stated.**

"I went to his 52nd St tour with my crush. I played that album over and over the day my crush got married to someone else two years later." **Patricia Alexander, location not stated.**

"Oh geez, I could probably write my own book. Every period of my life, every major event it seems, Billy Joel has been there for me. As a misfit kid, Just the Way You Are was an important song for me to hear. As a tween going through depression and social issues, I Go to Extremes helped me get to sleep at night. In high school, I would shout the lyrics to All For Leyna through the halls between classes. Every time I came home from college, I listened to Great Suburban Showdown on the airplane. Heck, when I quit my job this summer, on my last day of work I recorded myself singing Everybody Has a Dream and uploaded it for my boss and co-workers. Billy Joel is the soundtrack of my life, and I can't express how important that is to me." **Emily Mesch, Skagway, AK**

"Amazing Jon! My memorable up-close experience was when Maritime Music reserved two front-row seats for the 1996 Master Class at Trenton State College in NJ. Billy called on me to ask one of the final questions during that class. My question was pertaining to his song, Just the Way You Are, and how the song expressed the ideas of tolerance and understanding that have allowed me to triumph over cerebral palsy, like how a mom would sing that song lovingly to her child. I was talking into the microphone for about 20-25 seconds while looking down, as I felt too overwhelmed to look at my idol, Billy, as he was listening to me. When I finished my question and looked back up at Billy, he had a sense of pure inspiration on his face as he looked directly at me, apparently speechless, thinking for several more seconds about how to respond. What I remember best is that his answer satisfied me and he went over to the piano and belted out the first two or three verses of Just the Way You Are while tickling the ivories. He even started the song with my name: "Paul, don't go changin' ..." With tears streaming down my face, I was so happy and overjoyed at that moment! It was like living a fantastic dream. The next day, my moment with Billy was described in an article that appeared in the local paper, "Billy Joel Fulfills a Dream." **Dr Paul Stuart Wichansky, NJ**

"I first heard the piano man intro and solo in the song and loved the bluesy piano playing. I have been playing piano and keyboards for over 30 years and I was instantly drawn to Billy's music. I won a competition in Ireland on one of the top commercial stations as Ireland's biggest Billy Joel fan. I flew to JFK, was picked up by a limo (staying in the Beacon Hotel for four nights) with two tickets for MSG on his 65th birthday with sight-seeing tour of New York with dinner for two in the Empire Stake House. I am a songwriter and fulfilled a lifelong dream of having Richie Cannata play sax on one of my songs on my debut album." **Keith O'Connell, Dublin, Ireland**

"My first memories of actively listening to music were putting my older brother's copies of 52nd St and Glass Houses on the turntable over and over. I spent my first paper route money on The Nylon Curtain cassette and eventually went out and bought the Billy Joel Complete series for piano. With those books in hand I convinced my piano teacher to take a left turn from classical and help me try a few of his tunes during my lessons. Playing those songs got me thinking about writing my own songs. I eventually learned to write and record my own stuff, formed a band in college, and ended up as a successful jingle composer right out of school. I've written music for ads, TV networks and video games for 20 years now. At one point I co-wrote a very Billy-esque song with an ad guy that knew Richie Cannata and we got him in to solo on it. Nicest guy on earth. He signed my brother's copy of Glass Houses at the session. I've only recently returned to these records riding around with my nine year old daughter listening to the BJ channel on satellite. She loves the whole Streetlife Serenade album and seems fascinated, like I always was, about it because it seemed like it was overlooked when it came out. I can still plunk out some of Root Beer Rag and she loves that. My entire career has been making music and I have those first loves, those Billy Joel albums, to thank for lighting that fire in me."
Ravi Krishnaswami, New Haven, CT.

"First concert was in 1993 and had Just The Way You Are sung at our wedding. Invited Billy Joel but did not get a response, so we put a selfie of him on a stick for our photo booth. Have seen him in concert 27 times. At our wedding my groomsman and I sang Uptown Girl to my wife in the middle of the dance floor." **Chris Gman, location not stated.**

"Ok so here's the story....everyone who knows me knows I love Billy Joel more than any other fan alive right? Anyway the plan: NYC for the concert, stay over and next drive to Long Island to be a tourist and see the gorgeous quaint little towns...took our time leaving the city...drove over to Oyster Bay where his bike museum is to see his collection which is unreal, all the time joking that if I ever met him I could die tomorrow. Park the car walk around the corner to his shop and spot a familiar bike. I say to Jim I think that's his bike he is seen zipping around on commonly! As we get closer I said I don't think it his. We approach the door and it's open but the sign says closed. We see the very nice man who runs his shop and the woman who does the upholstery for his seats for his bikes and ask are you open? They say no but come on in and take a look! We walk in and start chatting and looking at the bikes. As I turn to start walking up one of the aisles I see a guy standing at the back of the shop and it was him!!! I lost it!! I cried like a baby and was shaking like a leaf! Almost fell to the floor, truly the meaning of knees buckling! Jimmy did most of the talking as I couldn't. When I finally spoke I said to Billy that he is the only person in the world that I've ever wanted to meet and he has no idea what it meant to me!! He said "Wow, you need to get out more often!" We all laughed and he was really humble and down to earth and genuine. His shop manager Alex was a super cool guy as well and asked us to come inside after and chat for about an hour. I never in my wildest dreams expected to meet my number one idol since I was a little girl and never had such luck ever in my life! My planets have aligned today and my bucket list is complete as far as I'm concerned! Thank you to my *incredibly cool hubby who loves me completely for going on this adventure with me even though he shakes his head at my craziness!"* **Lisa Esposito, location not stated.**

"You're My Home was my wedding song and we ended the night as we always end all celebratory nights (wedding, bar mitzvahs, big anniversaries, 50th birthday) with Piano Man. I owe meeting my wife to Billy. I met my wife while living in the Caribbean on the small island of St Kitts. I was playing piano at a hotel bar that she was visiting with her parents; mostly Billy Joel tunes. She said she too loved his music and that she had the newly released River of Dreams tape cassette (which was not available on the little island). She showed it to me, I gave her a hug, and 2 kids and over a quarter of a century later we are still together and we have tickets to see him on his birthday, May 9th. (We have seen him about 50 times; if you include Master Classes, lectures/interviews, appearances, Blue Note, 121212 concert, Central Park w/Garth, Millenium at MSG, both Shea Stadium Shows, etc etc." **Doug Cotler, location not stated.**

"In my opinion, his song You're My Home is his very best. If you have someone in your life, that you consider your ''home'' - well then you are truly blessed to have that person, your 'home', in your life. I am brought to tears whenever I'm lucky enough to hear this song live. In addition, I have so many great concert memories, including my very first concert during The Stranger tour at MSG. Billy came out to perform and dedicated NY State of Mind to the Mets! The crowd went wild! It was a special NY moment, and one that I have such a fond memory of. As a musician, I truly appreciate his support of music education in our school. The amount of time, energy, and his generous donations of pianos to schools is so critical to the support of music education. What a testimony to his beginnings at Hicksville High School. Any musician who gives back to the community is number one in my book!" **Rosemarie Mannarino Stauber, location not stated.**

"Billy's songs have gotten me through some tough spots in my life. When my husband was hired to photograph him during the filming of a documentary about the piano, I was happy to assist. I sat at Billy's feet with a reflector and told him what his songs have meant to me and he conversed with me like I was an old friend. His humble personality made such an impact on me. I make the pilgrimage to see him at Madison Square Garden at least once a year. I've seen him 15 times now; I have no desire to see anyone else in concert; it just won't compare to how Billy can turn a 20,000 person arena into an intimate piano bar. There's just no one else like him." **Dana Huntington-Smith, Maryland.**

"Billy Joel is my husband's idol. He has been to all his concerts together. We love Billy and yes, we got married a year ago on Halloween and our first dance was Captain Jack. My husband would love to meet him in person, just never happened yet." **Lila Wilson Burton, location not stated.**

"My husband and I have always been friends since 7th grade (when we went steady and then dated a short time in high school). We both went separate ways but stayed friends. Invited to his first wedding and we danced to Just The Way You Are. Fast forward 11 years, he finds me after his divorce, we start dating, get married and dance to— Just The Way You Are!! Been married 28 years!" **Donna Vercellone Luther, location not stated.**

"I'm 18 and I've been listening to Billy for years and to be honest I have never really felt like I fit in anywhere. I'm a bit of an 'Old Soul'. Billy's music is special to me because for every issue that I face in life there appears to be a song that references the same feeling. If I miss a friend I play a song like Temptation; If something doesn't go my way, a song like Keeping the Faith or A Matter Of Trust cheers me up. Billy's writing is timeless because his words come from his life, not what sounds cool or even what people will love. In other words he doesn't write songs to sell millions of records, he does it for himself and what he feels like creating." **Andrew Saugus, Massachusetts**

"I have loved Billy Joel as a songwriter and performer since my teens in the late 70s/early 80s but have come to appreciate him more and for different reasons over the years. I love his brutal honesty, that he mentors aspiring artists through his master classes and by fostering new talent, and that he doesn't wear his politics on his sleeve but makes a statement when it is appropriate (i.e. wearing of the yellow star after Charlottesville). He really is a "rock star" in so many ways other than his incredible musical talent. I love hearing him perform with his daughter, Alexa, and how much he loves and cares for his family. Billy Joel has "normalized" being bipolar, or manic-depressive, through his incredible song, Summer, Highland Falls as well as I Go to Extremes and his willingness to share his own struggle with being bipolar with all of us, which is inspirational to those of us who struggle with being bipolar." **Mimi Platt Zimmerman, Dallas, TX**

"Billy has always been in my life. I can remember from a young age listening to him and just knowing he was unique. It was like he was singing to me, his words so relatable. It took me awhile to jump into his discography but it was well worth it. He may just be a singer, a storyteller to some but he is so much more to me. He has given me the memory of singing along to You May Be Right with my dad on my way home from school. He helped me release my frustrations by listening to Angry Young Man. Made me feel on top of the world with All About Soul. I may have not been there in his prime, but I will be here for ages to come. He helped me love music again. And for Billy I am forever grateful." **Autumn Okuszka, Michigan.**

"When my oldest son, who was 10 at the time, heard Billy on the car radio in 1978, he said to me: "Mom, listen to this guy, I think you're going to like him". That was the start of a 40 year love affair. Also when Billy played in NJ, at the Brendon Byrne Arena in 1987, my husband and I took our oldest son and youngest son to see him. We have since lost our youngest son in a construction accident at 21. But I keep the memory of him at that show with

me. He was so excited to see Billy Joel live and he sang along in so many of his songs. We have been to 10 concerts and at every one I think about my son and his excitement at seeing Billy." **Linda Weissman from Gilbert, Az. Originally NY and NJ.**

"Billy's music got me through a tough time in my teen years. I had a cassette of both The Stranger and 52nd Street I'd play every day. In fall of 1984 I made a failed suicide attempt after some really bad times. I still played that tape even during the time in the psych ward of the hospital (and I had been aware of Billy's similar situation). I was surprised to hear You're Only Human that summer." **Timothy Markin, Erie, PA.**

"Billy was my favorite when I was little, mid to late 70s. First album I bought with my own money was An Innocent Man. For my 17th birthday, my boyfriend at the time gave me four of Billy's cassette tapes. Would love to be able to see him at MSG some-day. Love how he has always stayed true to himself and cares about the working people. His songs are about real things and people. Always listen to him when I need to feel better...always makes me happy. Just love him and his music!! Also, the song You're Only Human helps me get through the rough times...Billy reminds me it's okay if I am not perfect." **Marie Aldridge from Erie PA.**

"The first song I played for the girl who would become my wife was Only the Good Die Young, in my room in my fraternity house. Not particularly romantic but I served her champagne (and no, I didn't get her wasted). Out of respect for our guests, I put it on the "do not play list" at our wedding. We've been to quite a few shows, a couple with her mother, since then." **Steven Bergstein, Living in the Boston area but originally from Long Island, New York.**

"In 1993 my son Harley was in the children's hospital in Charleston SC. Harley was three at the time. I called the local radio station and had them play Goodnight My Angel on the radio to him. He loved it. Move forward three years, he was six years old. It was the last year he was with us. He told me the strangest thing, he said when he died I need to play the River Of Dreams at his funeral along with some other selected songs. He always loved Billy Joel about as much as I do. He passed away that year due to an accident. I know in my heart how much he loved music and that it was what got him through all the rough times in his short life. Every time I hear those songs it brings a smile to my face to remember my music man. Harley Nov.8 1991 to Oct 15 1998. Submitted by his mom, Lea Ann Lollis." **Lea Ann Lollis, North Augusta, SC.**

"I'm 19 years old and I've loved Billy Joel since I was five. He's my idol and my favorite musician of all time. I listen to his music just about every day. His music just speaks to me in a way that no one else's does. When I was little my dad would play The Stranger album in the car and we would watch the Essential Billy Joel DVD, and I was hooked. His music has gotten me through everything, and I don't know what I would do without it. I can't even pick a favorite song, I love them all! I collect Billy Joel memorabilia as a hobby which is so fun. I've seen him in concert five times now and I hope to see him more. My dream is to meet him so I can tell him how much I appreciate him and his music!" **Natalie Cellini, Pennsylvania.**

"Was chef of a restaurant in East Hampton NY back in 1995. Billy was a two-three time a week regular. We got very friendly and had many a dinner together. Also a huge connection between me and my wife. We met week before Yankees Stadium concert. Both saw the show separately but went back to the place we met after the show. Been together ever since. He's played a huge part in our life." **Christopher Gerage Hey, location not stated.**

"I grew up in the Bronx and moved to Kings Park on Long Island. I have followed Billy since he started and have always felt that he is singing directly to everyone." **Donna Schwartz. I now live in Wellington, Fl.**

"Billy Joel is my favourite artist. His was my first concert more than 30 years ago and since then seen him three times in Sydney. A few years ago, saw him at MSG - that was a dream come true." **Mary Rose Ghaleb Haiek, Sydney, Australia.**

"Billy Joel was my first love! Fell in love with him in 1977 at 15 years old. I also had Just the Way You Are as my wedding song!" **Carol Carter Godfrey, location not stated.**

"Two songs that resonate personally are You're Only Human and It's All about Soul. All About Soul's lyrics resonate with me specifically since our daughter Heather passed away. It will be two years ago this April. Those words remind me to think and feel the happy times we spent with her. We have been fortunate to see Billy Joel in concert, my favorites being when he was at Fenway Park and also when he performed with Elton John." **Joyce Michelle Cohen, location not stated.**

"Lord, where to start? My first true love in high school got me started on Billy in '77. Saw him at alumni gym at Appalachian State in Boone. Hooked ever since. And when I'm down and out he gets me through the tough times through his songs." **Edie Shell King, location not stated.**

"His concert was the first concert I was allowed to go to at the Garden. My dad arranged a box. Must have been 1984 for my 19th Birthday. I heard he and Christie broke up. I announced at our community center in Rockland that I wanted to meet him. That I would make him happy. My friends laughed at me." **Lisamarie Ostuni, location not stated.**

"I'm an only child. Billy's music helped me when I was lonely. Billy was my first crush and my first heartbreak when he married Christie Brinkley on my birthday, March 23. He was every bit of my growing up and my heart melts when my kids, ages 29, 25, 21 and 14 sing their hearts out to his music still. I have never been blessed to see him live, he is on my Bucket List. He will always be my most favorite and cherished memory!" **Kimberlie Aviles Taylor, location not stated.**

"When I was a child my mother had all his vinyls. Whenever I was grounded I would listen to all Billy Joel. He became, is now and will forever will be my favorite artist of all time. I know the words to all of his songs and Billy Joel is my go to songs for the shower and karaoke. My all-time favorite, it wasn't ever released, is Josephine. I'm not star struck by any means, but if I ever ran into him in the street, I think I'd be speechless and that's difficult for me. #billyjoelforlife." **Daniel DeNisco Jr from Brooklyn, NY.**

"He is just so incredibly talented. He also lived in Sag Harbor like me. I love every one of his songs. I just think the lyrics to Just The Way You Are are so beautiful!" **Tonya Spinelli, Sag Harbor.**

"He grew up in Nassau County, LI and hung out where my kids hung out. At the Village Green, Borderline, Levittown, Hicksville, and Bethpage along with Eddie Money who went to Island Trees HS. Billy went to Hicksville, HS. I guess they were rivals." **Liz Feeney O'Brien, location not stated.**

"I met my husband because of a Billy Joel quote on his aol profile. I also waited overnight for tickets to my first Billy Joel concert at Madison Square Garden." **Amy Harris, location not stated.**

"My husband and I waited all night in Phoenix to get tickets in 2014 and a few years before that. We were the oldest people in line and were first in line. I get handicap seats so we had to go to the venue. It was so much fun meeting all these young people in line." **Linda Weissman, location not stated.**

"Billy used to go out for coffee with my now deceased grandpa who worked for a courier service. And my grandpa used to go to his Oyster Bay office. My grandpa was a stickler and made Billy sign for the packages himself so Billy liked his perseverance and went out with him for coffee. I was already a fan. This is late 80's. Also I went to last dress rehearsal of Movin' Out and Billy pulled up on his bike from out East. I went to give him a high five. We locked eyes and he went to give it back to me. As our hands got close, some kid stuck his hand in between ours. Billy and I shared a smile and we both shrugged as he moved off." **Joe Finck, Wantagh, NY.**

"I named my Event Space Vienna after Billy. I've seen him 23 times in concert and met him at a concert sitting front row with my brother after bidding on the package for charity. The next day Billy text me, I almost crashed my car! Nicest most down to earth man. He had my cell because I gave him my business card the night before at his 99th concert at the Garden." **Matt Prince, Roslyn Heights, NY**

"Billy Joel has helped shape my entire career!" **David James Guidice, location not stated.**

"I discovered Billy Joel on FM radio in Vancouver, BC when Piano Man was released in 1973. I play piano, so of course, I naturally fell in love with his music. When he broke with The Stranger, it seemed the whole world had now discovered my secret. I was in awe that one person wrote the music and lyrics. Billy's songs are not merely songs, they are vignettes that take us away to another place and time. I've only seen him in concert seven times, every time he has played Vancouver since 1980. I wasn't able to see the Billy/Elton show, I just couldn't afford it at the time. I am proud to say I have been a fan for 46 years. My dream is to see him in concert at MSG. I would love to meet him, but not in a meet 'n' greet situation, my dream would be to sit at a piano with him and have him teach me a few things.

To me, he is the most important songwriter of the latter half of the 20th Century. He is our modern day Gershwin and is fully deserving of every award he has received." **Julie Sapera, location not stated.**

"*I am a huge Billy fan! Billy is the reason why I play piano and continued pursuing music. When I was in my early teens, I was ready to quit my piano lessons. I saw an interview with Billy and listened to all of his trials and doubts. I was very young and can't remember exactly what he had said to change my mind, but I can say for certain that if he hadn't passed into my life at exactly that moment, I wouldn't have taken the same path in life that I had chosen because of him! I appreciated (and still appreciate to this day) how he is just a normal person with normal problems like the rest of us. I eventually got my music university degree. I still write music, and I am now a teacher. Billy kept my love and passion of music alive, and I am forever indebted to him. Thank you, Billy, from the bottom of my heart!*" **Kirsty Husel, Quebec, Canada**.

"*I fell in love with Billy Joel in 1978 at the first of many shows! I was living in Tucson and I was 14. To say my house was difficult would be an understatement! Billy became my happy place and his music truly got me threw some seriously painful times! I'd spend every year in line for 30 hours to get front row. I met Billy in 1989 at a show in Albany. Someone I worked with knew one of his photographers and he got me back stage for two shows. I got guitar picks, one of Liberty's drum sticks and a picture with Billy Joel! I'm grateful he came into my life when he did! His music saved my life.*" **Carol Carrillo, location not stated.**

"*I'm 40 years old, from Houston, TX. I've always been a fan but more of a casual fan (i.e. I just knew the hits). Recently my 11 year old daughter discovered his deeper catalogue via the Sirius channel and kept insisting that I listen to it with her. Well, she ended up turning me into a diehard.*

I'm now obsessed with his music, and he is tied with Brian Wilson as her favorite artist. What makes it special is the fact that I discovered his best work thanks to her. Different in the fact that here's someone born in 2007 getting her middle aged dad into a classic rock artist. Usually it's the other way around!" **Billy Castillo, TX**.

"I've been a Billy Joel fan since high school. My first Billy show was at the Capital theatre in Passaic, NJ. Then another show at William Paterson College in 1977/1978. I stayed up all night to get first row for that show!! But my main story here is that three years ago I reconnected with a high school friend, Heidi Kirchner, who still lives in NJ, who I went to the Billy concert with in high school. Well she flew down here to Orlando and we went to the Billy show here. Now earlier this year I flew to NJ and we went to Billy's 100th show at Madison Square Garden. Along with Heidi, another high school friend, Cindy Haner, joined us for this show and my sister-in-law, Tara Herman, from Maine came down for that show. Old friends and family still getting together for these phenomenal shows!" **Terrie Herman, location not stated.**

"I have a few stories to share. I have seen Billy 97 times and met him a few times - the highlight was playing Honesty on stage on the piano while Billy sang - it was at a Q and A - it's on YouTube. I met him a few weeks earlier at a Q and A with Don Henley that year and told him it was my 73rd time seeing him at that point - Billy replies "You need to get out more often!". I said back "I do - I'm seeing you next Saturday and the next Sunday after that!" A funny time was at the Face To Face show here in 2002. I got up front and for some reason grabbed Billy's watch and he started cursing me out in front of 18,000 people!" **Howard Klein, location not stated.**

"I went to my first Billy Joel concert in 1990. It was then that I realized that I wanted to be like him. Two years later, I began piano lessons. I always wanted to play Billy's music at my lessons and my teacher always allowed me to go over the one hour that was allotted for the lesson because I enjoyed it so much. To this day, I still consider playing the piano a passion and I enjoy performing Billy's music. I continue to go to his concerts as much as possible. I have been to over 30 of Billy's shows." **Frank Dowd III, Smithtown, NY**.

"I've been a lifelong Billy fan. I remember at a young age often asking my parents who was singing if the radio was on. More often than not it was Billy. There were times though I confused Elton for Billy but hey I was like five or six. I am completely deaf in one ear. To me Billy sounds fantastic. I can only imagine what he sounds like with full hearing. Fast forward to when I was 12, my parents got me a ticket to see him at what was the Worcester Centrum. The concert was to be my first on 1/19/87. Just The Way You Are was my last dance song at my wedding. Since that day in 1987 I have seen him 16 more times. I have met his daughter Alexa and most of his band members at least once. I have yet to meet the man himself. I would love to thank him for his music and let him know how his music has gotten me through some pretty dark times. Billy's music has been a lifesaver to me." **Melissa Stuchins, MA**.

"My husband, Mike and I met Billy on the beach in Montauk, NY where he was living with Christie Brinkley at the time. He was looking at some real estate and Mike was in the business. I am a piano player and he was my idol so I was speechless. As I eventually regained my voice, we invited him to join as for a few beers at the local pub. We had a great afternoon. Today I often look for him to introduce him to my 97 year old Dad who is a jazz tenor saxophone player. Dad played duets with John Coltrane in the sixties

and I know they would hit it off. However, our meeting was 30 years ago so I'm not sure Billy would remember it." **Patricia DeRosa Padden, location not stated.**

"I used to work in same office that Billy's manager worked in. I would see him often. Well my birthday is Dec 20th. My friend and I were coming back from lunch and Billy was in the elevator with the building handyman. He was trying to give him tickets to his show at The Coliseum as a thank you for Christmas. The handyman threw the tickets back at him claiming he'd rather have a bottle instead. My friend told Billy that it was my 18th birthday. Billy turns to me and asks if it's true, and if I had plans. Of course I did, but said no. So he hands me the tickets and wishes me a Happy Birthday! Best gift ever!" **Linda Collins, Hicksville, NY**

"My first Billy Joel concert was Jan 18th 1984. The night of the concert was a big thing for me but my buddy Scott, who I was with, didn't really care. I got dressed up in a suit and sneakers. I stashed my camera body down my pants and Scott stashed the lens down his pants. We got through a light pat down at security and then headed into the restrooms at the Providence Civic Center to rebuild my camera. So the concert starts and we could only see the top of Billy's head. After a handful of songs billy gets up and goes into Don't Ask Me Why at a mike stand right in front of us. Then Billy waves us up, to get closer to the stage, (this is called releasing the audience-you may see it marked on the set lists) now we are leaning on the stage with people all around us. Scott is 6'4" and a short girl behind him couldn't see, so I offer her my shoulders, she climbs on, her friend wants to go up too and I turn to Scotty and he lifts this girl right up in one swoop then she decides to jump on stage. We put about six or seven girls on stage. They were popping up from the left, the right, everywhere! I started clicking my camera and a security guy grabbed me and made me expose my film, luckily he only got a

new roll and not the ones in my pocket. By the time Billy did Only The Good Die Young there must have been 15 or 20 woman who jumped on stage. I had a great night and made Scotty into a new fan for Billy. A few years later I went again to see Billy this time with my future wife. By the time Billy called the audience up we were right there, I started lifting girls up and the next thing you know my wife is up there kissing Billy Joel and I ran out of film! When Billy started Uptown Girl I held out my sunglasses, he grabbed them and put them on. They were brand new! Billy wore them before me." **Kevin Mocker**

To Don & Sharon
Cheers!

Billy Joel

Oyster Bay, New York, October 2018

Jon Brett

Milton Keynes

United Kingdom

MK4 1JZ

jonbrettuk@hotmail.com

Billy Joel

Oyster Bay

Long Island

New York

USA

May 2019

Dear Billy

So. What did ya think? Different, huh?

I'm confident you will have never read anything like this before about yourself, your life or your music and what your music means to people.

I hope you've enjoyed reading it as much as I have enjoyed researching and writing it.

In fact, Sharon and I have had a blast hanging out in Hicksville, Oyster Bay, Sag Harbor, New York City and other Long Island beauty spots meeting your band members past and present and other great people along the road.

I never set out to write your biography – what would be the point in me doing that? And I don't claim to be your biggest fan, or the most knowledgeable fan. I'm just an ordinary person who really, really enjoys your music.

But it doesn't have to end here. In fact, I'm already planning the updated edition. You know, the version where Sharon and I actually do hang out with you and Alexis at your Oyster Bay mansion, all singing around the piano together eating your favourite popcorn and pancakes before joining you in your helicopter to Madison Square Garden and watching your show from the side of the stage.

I know we'd have a laugh. Not the kind of false, showbiz laugh you might have with Jimmy Fallon, or that annoying Brit, James Corden, but a real, wholesome, spare me all the luvvie bullshit laugh you'd have with your mates down the bike shop.

Yes, I'd write about it. But you'd enjoy reading it.

Email me. My email address is above.

Best regards

Jon Brett

Manufactured by Amazon.ca
Bolton, ON

11022547R00120